ᒐ ᐊ᙮ᐤ

tawâw

# tawâw

## Progressive Indigenous Cuisine

## Shane M. Chartrand

### with Jennifer Cockrall-King

Foreword by Marlene and Laurie Buffalo

Photography by Cathryn Sprague

AMBROSIA

# CONTENTS

# A NOTE ON LANGUAGE

Right now, in Canada, *Indigenous* is the preferred term to indicate indigeneity and that which belongs to or touches First Nations peoples and cultures. *Aboriginal* is also a widely used term in Canada — though we are aware of the colonial associations with this word and that our communities are moving away from it. For the purposes of this book, we've kept to the original words used in conversation and direction quotations.

Additionally, while it may sound like basic information, this bears repeating: The Indigenous peoples of North America are not just one cultural or ethnic group. We are made up of over 630 separate First Nations Communities, affiliated with over 50 Nations, speaking over 50 Indigenous languages in Canada alone. Indigenous peoples live in a wide range of environments, from reservations to cities, from the rainforest climates of the West Coast to the polar deserts of the high Arctic, and from the grasslands and high plains of the Prairies to the coastal communities of the Maritimes. Indigenous peoples include those of us who are First Nations, those of us who are Métis, and those of us who are Inuit. As of the 2016 Canadian census, there are 1.6 million of us here, and we make up 4.9 percent of the total population.

# FOREWORD

*BY MARLENE AND LAURIE BUFFALO*
SAMSON CREE NATION, TREATY NO. 6 TERRITORY

*tawâw: Progressive Indigenous Cuisine* is not just another cookbook; it is a collection of healing, of nourishment, of sharing. It is a way to welcome others into our homes and our lives, to share and honour what has been carefully grown, selected, and curated with the intent to create amazing food at home.

Indigenous cuisine is tied very closely to *nêhiyâwiwin*: Plains Cree culture, traditions, teachings, principles, and value systems. Food is meant not only to nourish the spirit but also to heal. Animals have their own medicine lines, where they go to heal themselves by eating. Therefore, it is natural that our food should nourish us physically as well as help us to heal and to grow mentally, emotionally, and spiritually.

To preserve, maintain, and share Indigenous traditions requires self-reflection, self-discipline, and a focussed ambition to get it right. When Shane asked us, a mother–daughter team, to contribute to this collection, we were deeply honoured — honoured to be involved with this book but also to witness and revel in the successes, hustle, and authenticity that Shane brings to all of the spaces that he occupies.

MARLENE: When I first met Shane he reminded me of a shark — very tenacious, always moving and looking for innovative food preparation techniques. Where else does one get to sit with such a brilliant "shark" but in a setting where he has created room for meaningful, authentic, sincere moments of

# INTRODUCTION

*tawâw* [pronounced ta-WOW]:
Come in, you're welcome, there's room.

What does it mean to be an Indigenous person who is an executive chef in charge of his own professional kitchen and staff? What does it mean to have cooks from different Nations working for me, looking for guidance on how to express their ambitions, their dreams, and their identities through food? How do I create — one dish, one menu, one dinner at a time — a progressive Indigenous cuisine? Not an historical re-creation but a cuisine that reflects who I am and how I live with one foot in the Indigenous world and the other in the non-Indigenous world? I've been asking myself these questions for the past 10 years — half of my professional cooking career. *tawâw* is my personal record of exploring these questions through conversations, education, and cooking with family, friends, and the culinary community I am proud to be a part of.

My birth name is Shane St. John Gordon. But for the first three decades of my life, I didn't know this fact. I also didn't know the names of my birth parents or my home Nation. I was a part of a large group of Indigenous children in Canada who were taken from our biological parents, placed into foster care, and then put up for adoption from the early 1960s through to the mid-1980s—what is now known as the "Sixties Scoop." I was given up when I was a year and a half old and was in foster care for five years. Though I was so young, I remember being alone, moving from place to place, and I remember being hungry. In those early years I didn't have a lot of food. I wasn't starving, but I remember being hungry all the time. That's really my earliest memory.

When I was almost seven years old, I was moved to the home of Belinda and Dennis Chartrand. They fostered a lot of children over the years, but of all the kids who went through their house, they chose to adopt me. I'm one of the lucky ones because I have an incredible and loving family. My mom, Belinda, is of Irish and Mi'kmaw descent. My dad, Dennis, is Métis. I have an older sister, Rae; an older brother, Ryan; and a younger sister, Erin. It took me a while to get to know my siblings, as I was the only adopted child in the family. This is how I came to have a Métis family.

With my dad, Dennis, and mom, Belinda, at REDx talks in Enoch, Alberta, in 2018.

**I LOVE KIDS.** I came from a family of 10 children, and I knew early on that becoming a foster parent and adopting were my calling.

For the most part, Shane was a really good kid, though he threw temper tantrums for months after he first arrived in our home. He was already six and a half and he'd been passed around quite a few times. He was probably worried that he wasn't staying, so he was really testing us. At bedtime, he'd scream and kick the walls. He didn't want to go to bed. And after he was done with the tantrum, he'd call me to say, "Mom, I need my goodnight kiss."

One night he said to me, "Mom, when I first came you told me that you were so glad that I was your boy. Are you still glad I'm your boy?" I told him yes, I was, and that he'd always be our boy.

Other than the tantrums, he fit right in to the family and he made friends quickly. He helped around the house, butchering, cleaning, plucking. He would work all day. And he always had a smile on his face. He was just a happy-go-lucky kid.

About a year after he started working at the restaurant truck stop on the highway, Dennis and I went there for lunch. We wanted to see what he was actually doing. You know those racks with all those order chits they attach to them and it spins around? Well, he was working his way through the orders, making one dish after another. He'd never been a coordinated child. He couldn't even chew gum and tie his shoes at the same time. It was amazing to watch him doing that so efficiently.

— Belinda Chartrand

Me at about age seven (*right*) with my cousin Denny Marchand in Penhold, Alberta.

Our home was on an acreage midway between the cities of Calgary and Edmonton, in the province of Alberta. I went to River Glen School, a public school in Red Deer. I was the only Indigenous kid at the school. There was one black kid and one Mexican kid, but I was the only kid who identified as "Aboriginal"—the word we were using in those days.

As a family, we sat around the table and ate dinner together every night. It wasn't what I was used to from my time in foster care. That might seem sad for some, but it wasn't for me since I didn't know better until I got adopted. Only then was I introduced to good food, sitting with family, and rules.

My mom's cooking was very simple, but keep in mind there could have been 10 or 12 foster kids living with us at any time, and my dad was often on the road for work. Mom used to cook up big pots of stew, chili, and soup. I loved her goulash, cabbage rolls, and spaghetti and tomato sauce. And she made this really great pistachio pudding dessert with whipped cream and marshmallows that I absolutely adored, too. It was so "of its time" but pretty damn delicious. My mom likes to tell me that I always said "thank you" after each meal—and that I was the only kid at the table who did.

My dad went hunting a lot—so much so that we got sick of eating moose meat! Mom and Dad had about five or six acres of land. We had a barn and a long log home. There were horses, chickens, ducks, rabbits, and geese on the property. And there was a beautiful farmer's field behind the house. Nowadays, I would build a cob oven or smokehouse there, but Mom and Dad sold the property a number of years ago. It was a lot for them to keep up.

So much happened in that back field—everything from Dad teaching me how to drive our van, to just being a kid doing ridiculous kid-things, to simple gardening. Oh, the amount of gardening we did was just incredible!

We grew turnips, potatoes, carrots, onions, and rhubarb—normal stuff, nothing crazy. And we had a beautiful root cellar that my dad, my brother Ryan, and I built together. Mom did a lot of pickling. You'd walk in the house and the smell of vinegar would be so strong. She made the best pickles ever. (Of course, right?)

I guess you'd say Dad grew up poor. His family's house didn't have any electricity and there was only an outhouse for a bathroom. So his big thing was saving money and being frugal. He's retired now, but in his working life he was a mechanic and a welder. He can fix anything. He built a chicken-plucking machine. Our garage always contained a vehicle he was working on. He'd be replacing an engine, and there would be a deer hanging right beside the car, ready for butchering.

We raised geese, ducks, and chickens on our acreage. It was always my job to chop their heads off. I didn't realize it until I was older, but my dad is actually a really emotional guy. I didn't see that because he was also very strict

In the woods north of Edmonton, Alberta.

and serious. It was only as an adult that I figured out Dad made me slaughter the birds because he couldn't do it.

When we went hunting, it was always about getting food for the table. It had nothing to do with taking pictures and proving who is the coolest hunter, like it is today. Through hunting, Dad started teaching me about our culture. He'd tell me, "I need your roots to always be there as an Aboriginal, and I'll do the very best I can to make sure that you are in touch with your First Nations' ties."

One of the things I love most about my dad is that he has great hunting stories, even when he exaggerates them a touch. And some of my favourite memories as a kid are when Dad would take me on long "survival" trips. They could be anywhere from two weeks to a month. (Two weeks really isn't a survival trip, but one month certainly is.)

When I was 16 years old, Dad took me and my cousin on a trip to the mountains for a few weeks. Dad made us pack on our own, but he inspected our packs in secret and then hid the things that we'd forgotten in the Jeep. (The idea was to teach us how to pack properly and be self-sufficient. Did we have the right knife? Not the biggest knife, not the smallest or lightest

**I GREW UP IN A LITTLE TOWN** called Hillcrest, in the Crowsnest Pass in Southern Alberta. My dad used to take me fishing and hunting all the time — big game hunting. That's how I learned to skin and butcher animals. We lived off the land because money was scarce. I used to shoot and bring home rabbits and stuff when Dad was off working in the mines.

My mom made her own breads and bannock. She made all types of stews, using rabbit or whatever meat we had on hand. I grew up with all the wild foods and game, like deer and moose (and I just carried on doing that with my own family). All the kids knew what it was like to go out hunting or to start skinning a deer in the garage and how to butcher it.

I used to take Shane and his cousin Denny on what I called "survival trips." They were 9 or 10. At that age, it used to take some fifteen .22 shells to bring down a grouse. Shane was not first-rate with a gun in those days!

I still like to go hunting, fishing, and travelling. My sister likes to hunt, so we go together.

But I also like to be alone in the bush. It gives me a sense of serenity. I feel relaxed out there. I'm just closer to everything. Things have changed a lot in my lifetime. I remember the streams and creeks where we used to fish. They were full of little brook trout. All you needed was an empty hook and they'd bite it. The fishing is getting harder now. There aren't the fish there used to be. And the size — they're nothing now. The deer are getting more used to humans, so there's not much sport in hunting them. The moose are still elusive but there seems to be fewer of them as well, and they're harder to find.

Still, my favourite food is a good-old slough-fed moose: a nice moose steak cooked outdoors over an open fire, with lots of potatoes. Shane made that last year when we were out hunting. I've told him that some of his fancy dishes wouldn't feed a chickadee. I also told him long ago that he's got to find his roots. That's where he came from, so that's what he needs to learn more about.

— Dennis Chartrand

knife, but the *right* knife?) We spent three weeks out in the mountains and ate goofy things. I remember him teaching us how to cook squirrel over a fire.

When I was younger, I wanted to be a cabinetmaker. I also wanted to be an actor, an artist, or really anyone in the visual arts. Cooking as a career happened sort of by chance.

When I was about 14, I asked my mom for money to buy something ridiculous—as kids do—like a pair of sneakers. Her response was that I could buy whatever I wanted but first I'd have to find a job. So I jumped on my bicycle and rode out to the highway and applied for the first job I could find. I started as a dishwasher at a 60-seat truck stop attached to a gas station called Pumper's Cafe. A year and a half later, I was promoted to short order cook. I'm very proud to have worked at a truck stop—most of the menu items were made from scratch—and it was a lot of fun. It's where my career started. It's a part of my history.

I tried to impress my parents with my cooking skills, but Mom and Dad didn't really like me cooking at home in those days. I wasn't all that good, to be honest. I was really just starting out. I wanted to learn more. But there was no Food Network. And I was often trying to make things that were beyond my skill level. I knew I wanted to get better. That said, it took me years just to get good.

I dated a girl for three or four years when I was quite young and skinny (I weighed 120 pounds at 18 years old). Her mom was a great cook. She made sure we sat down every day to eat together, even though I was just the boyfriend. What impressed me most was that nothing repeated during the week! This is how little I knew about cooking at the time—planning a series of meals that didn't repeat was a revelation. I remember thinking, *Did she seriously go to the store and plan the whole week of meals? How do you plan that?*

When I moved from the acreage to Edmonton, there was a lot of talk in the food world about "eating local." I didn't understand what that meant because at my parents' home, that was a normal thing. It was what I had to do on Saturdays: work in the garden, kill the chickens, kill the geese, kill the ducks. My family taught me to have a lot of respect for food when we'd go hunting    don't waste it, don't throw anything away.

I circled back to this concept later in my career, but in my early twenties I was working in chain restaurants, busy places that served burgers, fries, nachos, that sort of thing. I still didn't know enough about food and cooking. I remember a trip that my then-girlfriend and I took to Las Vegas. I wanted to go to a "super-fancy" restaurant, so we chose to go to Picasso, the French restaurant at the Bellagio, which had just opened and was later awarded two Michelin stars. My date and I sat there eating little bits and bites. We let the waiter pick our wine selection for us because I knew nothing about wine. We had two servers to ourselves, and there was only the two of us. There was some guy just waiting to fill our water. We sat on the veranda overlooking the fountains and the water show. I was completely out of my league. I had no clue what I was eating. I had no idea how complex it was or how hard it was to make food like that. I didn't even understand the creativity involved. I was so naive.

I kept cooking—mostly in chain restaurants—and worked my way up through professional kitchens. I became a kitchen manager. But as I approached my mid-twenties, I started to realize that staff who were younger than me, who looked up to me for leadership, knew more about food than I did. My math wasn't the greatest and I hadn't really been taught much because I was promoted ahead of my skill level simply because of my work ethic.

It's an uncomfortable position to be in, when you feel you're supposed to be at a certain level and you know you aren't there. It was especially difficult when I was running a place and I knew the cooks were better than me. I couldn't give them any guidance. I couldn't help or coach them. All I could do was lie.

I decided I needed to get out of chain restaurants, where I really only learned how to follow instructions, not cook. It worried me. I didn't want to wake up one day and not know anything about the fundamentals of cooking. So at 23 years of age I enrolled in culinary school—but I only completed the first year before a divorce and some family things meant I had to go back to work full time.

Plating up for dinner service in my kitchen at River Cree Resort & Casino in Enoch, Alberta.

I started work at a hotel and began all over again as a garde manger, an entry-level kitchen job making salads and other basic dishes. I also did banquets. I did every kitchen job I could to get myself back on track. Only this time I decided I needed to work my way up properly.

I got to write my first menu at a restaurant called Dezio's. I was a kitchen manager and chef there. I was also chef at a Lebanese restaurant, where I learned to make dolmades, fattoush, and shakriya, which is a hot yogurt stew. That job impressed upon me the importance of food in a larger cultural context. We'd go to the owners' house for these huge feasts—enormous gatherings where everyone's kissing and hugging, drinking wine, having fun, getting drunk, smoking cigars, eating a ton of food, and talking in their native language. It was like nothing I had experienced before. And it was all combined with music, art, culture, and dancing.

Me at 19, displaying my artistic "chaud froid" project (a cooked dish that's made, cooled, and glazed in aspic or gelatin) at culinary school, in Edmonton.

Finally, I returned to culinary school and graduated. In 2006, I was hired as executive sous-chef at Sage, a fine dining restaurant at the River Cree Resort & Casino, a then-new operation on the Enoch Reservation on the western edge of Edmonton. It was an expensive, Las Vegas–style steak and seafood place where you paid extra for every side on your plate. It worked because it was one of the only new restaurants to open in Edmonton that year.

After two and a half years, I left Sage to work at another restaurant, Dante's Bistro. One night a man from the Enoch band recognized me. He asked, "What is your earliest memory?" I told him I was adopted and didn't know where I was born or who my biological parents were. All I had was a photo of me as a toddler with two other kids. There were three names written on the back: Shane, John, and Gordon. I assumed that those were the names of the three of us in the photo.

"No, those are your names," he explained. "I am your first cousin. You are from Enoch, and your name is Shane John Gordon. You're from the Gordon clan." (The "St. John," I was told, came about later because I loved going to church when I was very little. I also learned that my biological mother, Gloria Gordon, was from Enoch, where I now work and have my own restaurant.

In a strange way, I've come full circle in my life because of my career.) Finally, I had an anchor for my identity. I was Plains Cree from the Enoch Nation. But I still had a lot to learn and I didn't even know where to begin.

After Dante's Bistro, I was hired as executive chef at a restaurant called L2 in Edmonton. It was an Asian-inspired restaurant, and I started learning about a whole new category of ingredients. It was a very creative time for me. I was given very little direction from the management, and they let me and my staff experiment as much as we wanted. We'd go off to an Asian grocery store that was in the same shopping mall—okay, not just *any* shopping mall; it was West Edmonton Mall, the largest shopping centre in the world at the time—and buy live eels, geoduck, and whatever else we could get our hands on. Then we'd cook them up for our staff meals.

I became very interested in Susur Lee, a Canadian chef who was world famous for the Asian-fusion cuisine he served in his restaurants in Toronto. Understanding how Susur was able to incorporate his Hong Kong and Chinese cultural influences in a modern Canadian context was a light-bulb moment for me. He made me realize that there was a way for me to discover Indigenous foods and ways of cooking through my own interpretations.

One day at L2 I cooked for a delegation of 20 people from the Navajo Nation. I served a seven-course upscale menu that involved a saddle of rabbit and a higher-end version of bison tartare, along with some other dishes. I felt really great about the menu and the food—something clicked inside me. It was so exciting. And my food made them so incredibly happy that I knew I had to keep going.

I returned to Sage in 2013, this time as executive chef, and within a few years the restaurant was remodelled and rebranded as SC—for Shane Chartrand. Since the very beginning, I have found the work environment and community at the River Cree Resort & Casino to be incredibly supportive. I've been able to organize dinners that showcase my ideas around progressive Indigenous cuisine, and we have many Indigenous and Indigenous-inspired items that regularly rotate through the menu.

When I first began talking about progressive Indigenous food, most people were puzzled. What does that mean? How are you going to do that? How is contemporary Indigenous cooking different from mainstream Canadian cooking? How is it the same?

A lot of my cooking is mainstream—dishes that use classic European techniques and global ingredients. But the more I explore my Indigenous roots and develop my vision of progressive Indigenous cooking, the more

With the amazing Enoch Reservation community garden crew:
(*left to right*) Sabrina and Sweet Morin, Jesse Woodland, and Kyle Hebert.

people from all walks of life are excited about what a First Nations perspective can bring to the plate. In my culinary journey, I am trying to get to know myself better. But I also want to know more about Indigenous cultures and communities. So where do I start?

Well, I started by talking to Elders, to people from my own Nation—by sticking my nose in where it doesn't belong and by listening. I still feel like an outsider a lot of the time and I work hard to make connections so that I gain the trust of people who can teach me what I need to know—to try to put the pieces together. Now wherever I travel, I try to connect with local Nations. I've become bolder about that sort of thing. I want to learn more about different cultures in the Indigenous world. I continue to think, learn, listen, and create as I hone in on what progressive Indigenous cooking means to me. How can I make First Nations food exciting? How can I write a book that you just can't put down? As I've been thinking about these things, I said yes to every television appearance, speaking engagement, and event where I could learn something new or expose my ideas to a wider audience.

For instance, in 2015 I appeared on a competitive cooking show called *Chopped Canada*, where I dedicated my participation to my mom and dad as a big public thank-you for adopting me. Winning the competition wasn't as important to me as inspiring Indigenous kids to do something that they might not have considered before—to go to culinary school, to be a restaurant manager, to be a chef, to be on a television show. I certainly didn't grow up seeing faces in mainstream media that reflected how I looked and where I came from. So for me, the most important part of my presence on *Chopped Canada*, and any other television and documentaries I do, is representation. What keeps me going is the realization that the more I talk, the more people listen. There's a lot of momentum. At the end of the day, it's my contribution, my way of helping. If people are still interested, I'll keep talking.

My thinking on progressive Indigenous cuisine has evolved since I started on this journey 10 years ago, and I imagine it will continue to expand and grow. But I feel like I finally have a good, clear idea of what feels authentic and exciting, not just to me but to more and more people who are excited by the exploration of Indigenous perspectives in food.

That said, if I was going to celebrate only Indigenous people and purely Indigenous ingredients and cooking techniques in my cookbook, it would go against everything that I am doing at my restaurant. At SC, I often use

Beets and edible flowers on bison shoulder blade.

European and Asian cooking techniques. I love coriander seed. I do a lot of pickling. For me, it's about making something new and interesting out of various influences. In other words, I didn't want this book to be just about me and only about the First Nations side of me. Sure, it's about my life, my recipes, what I like to cook and eat, where I like to travel. It's about finding those information bundles that we all can share and learn from. After all, food is a place where the Indigenous and non-Indigenous worlds can easily connect. Whether you have Indigenous ancestors or not, everyone in North America should be learning about the First Nations' cultures that surround them. For my part, I can share recipes that I've created or learned, relay stories, and highlight the creativity of my Indigenous world through food.

The idea is to bring the beauty and artistry of my world to everybody. The more I expose people to my culinary ideas, the more people want to know. I know people are interested in Indigenous ways of thinking and of dreaming up dishes. But please remember, this book is my personal culinary story. I'm not trying to represent anything other than what I've been working on for the past decade—that is, learning how to create dishes that express my personality, learning about my own identity and history, and ultimately dreaming about our future together in a way that inspires the next generation of cooks—Indigenous or otherwise—to explore their own stories through food.

I offer this book as a contribution to the wider conversation about Indigenous cultures and peoples from my own unique perspective through food. It is my dream that this book ignites the imaginations of a new generation to discover what it means to cook, eat, and share food in our homes, in our communities, and in our restaurants. *tawâw*'s larger mission is to embrace a massive positive message about Indigenous cultures, something that we don't hear nearly enough about in North America. In other words, if you aren't from the Indigenous world or the culinary world, this book is still very much for you! I want everyone to be able to experience the beauty of the land and people around us, and the food that we can create with it.

Dream with me.

*Shane Chartrand*

# A NOTE ABOUT COOKING TIMES AND HEAT SETTINGS

The recipes in this book have been written for and tested using domestic home appliances, and the oven temperatures recommended assume you are using the convection setting on your oven. Because every stove and oven performs slightly differently, we have included indicators for "doneness" in each recipe — that is, visual and aromatic cues for each stage of cooking. Use these descriptions as your primary guide, adjusting the heat and cooking times as needed for your oven and stove. If you don't have a convection setting, you may need to either cook the dish a little longer or increase the oven temperature by 25°F / 4°C. When cooking and roasting meats, it's best to rely on a good oven-safe thermometer to determine the precise internal temperature of whatever you are cooking.

A long-table dinner under the Saamis Tepee in Medicine Hat, Alberta.

ᐧ ᐃᕆᐳᐟ

*pê-mîcisok*

COME AND EAT

ᒥᔪᐢᑲᒥᐣ

*miyoskamin*

# SPRING

# SPRING

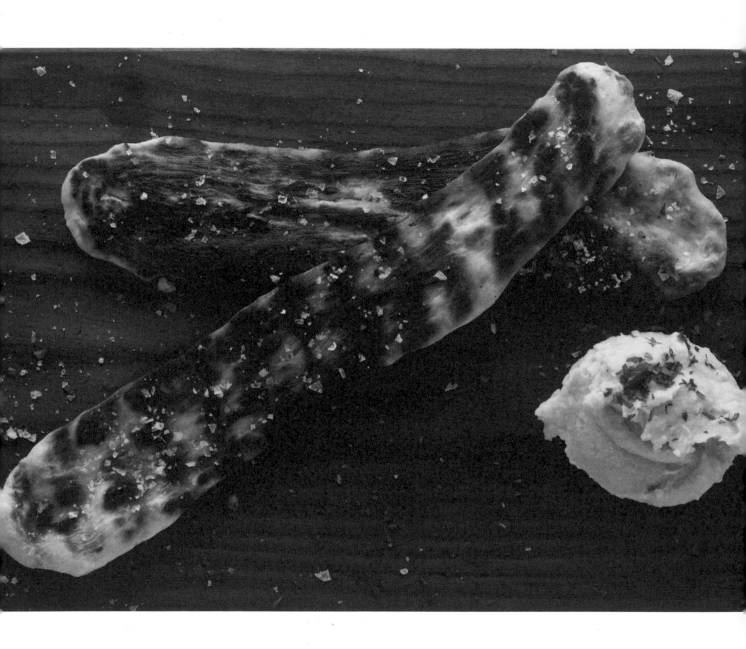

# WHITE BEAN DIP

MAKES 4 TO 6 SERVINGS

I just love the creaminess of white beans and the fresh hit of gingerroot in this recipe. Yes, there's a bit of cream, but the protein-rich beans make this such a healthy and satisfying snack. Put it out for guests or your family to nibble on just before dinner. Serve with Bannock (recipe page 286).

1   Place the beans in a large pot and cover in cold water. Let soak overnight. Drain and then rinse under cold running water. (If you forget to do this, pour boiling water over the beans in the pot and let soak for an hour or so, and then proceed with the recipe.)

2   Combine the soaked beans, garlic, broth, rosemary, and ginger in a medium saucepan over medium heat. Bring to a low boil. Reduce the heat to low, cover, and simmer for an hour or until the beans are quite soft. Discard the rosemary stems and ginger. Using a colander, strain well, reserving the cooking liquid.

3   Transfer the strained beans and garlic to a blender. Add the cream and purée until smooth. Add as much of the reserved liquid as you need to reach your desired consistency. Using the back of a wooden spoon, pass the purée through a fine-mesh sieve into a bowl. Season to taste with salt and, if you like, white pepper.

1 lb / 450 g dried cannellini (white kidney) or dried great northern beans

2 tbsp / 30 mL finely minced garlic

8 cups / 2 L Pheasant Broth (recipe page 280) or good-quality chicken broth

1 sprig fresh rosemary

1-inch / 2.5-cm piece fresh gingerroot, peeled and cut into ¼-inch / 0.5-cm chunks

¼ cup / 60 mL whipping (35%) cream

Salt and freshly ground white pepper, to taste (optional)

# GARLIC NETTLE DIP

MAKES 3 CUPS / 750 ML | SPECIAL EQUIPMENT: THICK GLOVES FOR HANDLING NETTLES

This recipe makes a fair amount of dip, but you'll want to make lots of it in the spring when the nettles are so abundant and healthy. Freeze half for a cooler day when you're baking fresh bread, Galette (recipe page 209), or Bannock (recipe page 286) and crave that tonic of green nettles and spicy garlic.

This also works as a delicious sauce for pasta with a generous amount of Parmesan cheese shaved on top.

1   Bring a large pot of salted water to a boil. Prepare an ice water bath (a large bowl filled with cold water and ice cubes).

2   Carefully add the nettle leaves to the boiling water and stir for 30 seconds or so to submerge them. Using a slotted spoon, transfer the blanched nettles to the prepared ice bath. Using your hands, gently squeeze out any excess water and transfer the blanched nettles to a blender (reserve the ice water bath). Set aside.

3   Fill a small pot with 2 inches / 5 cm of cold water. Add the garlic and bring to a simmer, then cook for about 30 seconds. Drain and discard the hot water. Repeat and simmer the garlic for another 30 seconds. Drain and repeat one more time. Transfer the blanched garlic to the ice water bath and let cool for 30 seconds.

4   Place the cooled garlic in the blender with the nettles. Add the oil, water, lemon juice, shallots, and salt. Purée until smooth. Taste and adjust the seasoning, if necessary.

2 cups / 500 mL densely packed stinging nettles, leaves only (about 1.2 oz / 35 g)

1 head of garlic, separated into cloves and peeled

2 cups / 500 mL cold-pressed canola oil

1 cup / 250 mL water

¼ cup / 60 mL fresh lemon juice

¼ cup / 60 mL minced shallots

¼ tsp salt

**STINGING NETTLES** (*Urtica dioica*) are no joke. You'll quickly learn to wear heavy gardening gloves, thick pants, and long sleeves when picking them, as their tiny hairlike barbs will cause an itchy, burning rash that can last for several hours if they come into contact with bare skin. Stinging nettles grow in waist-tall to head-high thickets in low-lying, moist, recently disturbed, rich soil. They are less difficult to handle in the early spring when the growth is still somewhat tender but become quite prickly as they shoot up in the summer.

I figure any plant with that kind of defense system must be a goldmine of nutrition. And it is! Rich in vitamins, minerals (especially calcium and iron), and protein, you can use cooked nettles as a spinach substitute in soups and stir-fries.

# KALE AND TOASTED PUMPKIN SEED SALAD

MAKES 2 SERVINGS

Seeds are small miracles, the hope of springtime. And it's no accident that I chose pumpkin seeds for this salad. We have been growing *Cucurbita*, the scientific name for the genus that includes squash, pumpkin, and gourds — along with corn and beans — for thousands of years. This is a vibrant salad, from the bright greens and purples of the kale to the sharp tang of the lemon in the dressing. Frying half of the kale gives it crunch, and blanching the other half tenderizes, providing a nice contrast.

1   *Make the salad:* Bring a large pot of salted water to a rapid boil. Prepare an ice water bath (a large bowl filled with cold water and ice cubes).

2   Submerge about one-quarter of the kale leaves and all of the Brussels sprout leaves and green onions in the boiling water. Cook for about 30 seconds (you want the leaves to be tender but still resilient). Using a wire-mesh scoop or slotted spoon, transfer the blanched greens to the prepared ice water bath and submerge for about 30 seconds. Scoop out the cooled greens, shake off any excess liquid, and pat dry with a clean cloth or paper towel. Set aside.

3   Preheat a deep-fryer to 350°F / 180°C or pour about 3 inches / 7.5 cm of oil into a deep pot. (If you have a wire-mesh splatter screen for the top of the pot, it will soon come in handy.) Line a baking sheet with paper towel.

4   Immerse the remaining kale leaves in the hot oil (make sure the leaves are very dry so the oil won't splatter too much). At first it will bubble vigorously, but as the moisture cooks out, there will be less activity. Fry until the leaves turn medium brown around the edges, about 20 seconds (the leaves should be crunchy but still flexible). Using a wire-mesh scoop or slotted spoon, scoop out the leaves and give them a gentle shake over the deep-fryer. >>

## FOR THE SALAD

1 lb / 450 g baby kale leaves, divided

20 Brussels sprout leaves (from about 2 Brussels sprouts)

6 green onions, green parts only, cut into 1.5- to 2-inch / 4- to 5-cm lengths

Neutral-flavoured cooking oil (such as canola), for frying

½ tsp / 2.5 mL fleur de sel plus extra for seasoning

2 tbsp / 30 mL unsalted raw pumpkin seeds

## FOR THE DRESSING

2 tbsp / 30 mL cold-pressed canola oil or extra-virgin olive oil

1 tbsp / 15 mL finely grated lemon zest

Juice of ½ lemon

¼ tsp / 1 mL salt

5   Turn the leaves out onto the prepared baking sheet.
    Season with the fleur de sel. Set aside.

6   In a dry cast iron or heavy sauté pan over medium
    heat, toast the pumpkin seeds just until light golden.
    Transfer toasted seeds to a plate.

7   *Make the dressing:* Whisk together the oil, lemon zest,
    lemon juice, and salt in a small bowl.

8   To serve, combine the deep-fried kale and your
    blanched greens in a bowl. Drizzle with the dressing
    and gently toss to coat all of the greens. Turn out
    onto a nice platter and top with the toasted pumpkin
    seeds. Finish with a sprinkling of fleur de sel.

## COLD-PRESSED OILS

On the Canadian Prairies, we're lucky to have producers of certified organic
non-GMO cold-pressed canola, flax, and hempseed oils. These freshly
pressed oils — pay attention to the expiry date when purchasing — are
extruded gently from the seeds without the use of heat or solvents common
in most edible oil production. Cold-pressed canola oil has an incredible nutty
aroma and flavour, plus an extraordinary colour reminiscent of sunflowers.
Cold-pressed flax oil has a buttery and slightly nutty flavour, with a golden
colour. Cold-pressed hemp oil is dark green and tastes of freshly mown grass
(in a good way!). Once open, store cold-pressed oils in the fridge and use
within about 4 months. These are finishing oils, full of colour, flavour, and
nutrition.

# EGGS WITH CAVIAR AND BANNOCK

MAKES AS MANY AS YOU LIKE | SPECIAL EQUIPMENT (OPTIONAL): IMMERSION CIRCULATOR MACHINE; 7-QUART / 6.6-L LEXAN CONTAINER (SEE SIDEBAR ON PAGE 31)

Are sous vide eggs part of Indigenous cuisine? Why not. It's a contemporary version of cooking eggs in their shell on hot ashes. The addition of fish roe and bannock make this an elegant dish with an authentically Indigenous feel.

Sous vide eggs, done properly, seem to demand a lot of work (and equipment), but they really are the softest eggs you'll ever have. The whites of fresh eggs will set up best. If you don't have the equipment to sous vide the eggs, you can simply poach them. And caviar — well, why not?

1   *Make the bannock:* Follow the instructions on page 286. Wrap the bannock in a clean cloth to keep warm.

2   *Meanwhile, sous vide the eggs:* Follow the instructions on page 31 to sous vide your eggs. Alternatively, you can poach the eggs just before serving: Bring a pot of water and splash of white vinegar to a gentle boil. Carefully crack in the eggs and cook for 3 minutes. Using a slotted spoon, remove the eggs from the water (give the spoon a gentle tap to shake off any excess moisture).

3   Serve the warm eggs individually in small cups or bowls. Top with the caviar and some smoked sea salt. Serve with a slice of warm bannock.

Bannock (recipe page 286)

Fresh large eggs (as many as you like)

White vinegar

½ tsp / 2.5 mL caviar of your choice (preferably Ocean Wise) per egg, for serving (see Tip)

Smoked sea salt, for garnish

---

TIP

I like to use sustainably farmed Ocean Wise sturgeon (black) caviar from a Canadian company called Northern Divine (they ship within Canada and to the United States). Alternatively, talk to your local seafood purveyor about other sustainable sources of caviar. You can find a good listing of sustainable caviar varieties and sources at ocean.org.

# How to Sous Vide Eggs

Fill a Lexan container* with water until it sits between the "min" and "max" water level indicator of your immersion circulator wand. Preheat the water to 145°F / 63°C (follow the manufacturer's instructions). Using a slotted spoon, gently submerge the eggs (in their shells) and cook for 2 hours. You can make the eggs up to 5 days ahead and keep them in the refrigerator.

If you're making the eggs ahead of time, it's important to chill them rapidly right out of the immersion circulator bath. To do this, make an ice water bath and transfer them directly from the hot water of the immersion bath to the ice water bath. Let them cool for at least 20 minutes before draining and refrigerating. An hour or so before serving, take them out of the refrigerator and bring them to room temperature.

Just before serving, bring a pot with about 2 inches / 5 cm of water to a gentle boil and add a splash of vinegar. Take the eggs from the immersion circulator bath, gently crack the shells, and slide the whites and yolks carefully into the boiling water for 20 seconds. (This will firm up the whites just enough without further cooking the yolk.) Remove them with a slotted spoon and gently tap the spoon to shake off any excess water. If making Eggs with Caviar and Bannock, continue with next step of the recipe on page 29.

* The best sous vide container, to me, is made of Lexan — a type of hard, non-porous food-grade plastic favoured by the commercial food industry. Cambro and Rubbermaid, among other brands, make them.

# OYSTERS ON A BEACH

MAKES 2 TO 4 SERVINGS (AS AN APPETIZER) | SPECIAL EQUIPMENT: OYSTER KNIFE

I was 26 years old when I ate my first raw oyster. (Remember, I'm a Prairie kid from a small town. Oysters were not part of my world when I was growing up or even when I was a young chef.) My girlfriend at the time was writing her American nursing exam in Coeur d'Alene, Idaho. We stayed at a casino and ate at the restaurant there called Crickets. I ordered the oysters and was immediately hooked. It was such a social way of eating that it became my go-to night out with friends — like going out for chicken wings, but a step up.

1   *Make the "beach":* In a large bowl, combine the kosher salt and lava salt. Stir in the water until well combined (it should be the consistency of beach sand: not very wet, but holding together). Turn it out into a serving dish and smooth until it's mostly level.

2   *Shuck the oysters:* Using your oyster knife, open each oyster and detach the foot. Discard the top shell but keep the oyster and its liquid in the "cup," or bottom half of the shell. (For shucking tips, see page 36.)

3   Drizzle each oyster with about ¾ tsp / 3 mL of the oil. Place each shell into the "beach" and serve immediately.

2 cups / 500 mL coarse kosher salt

2 cups / 500 mL black lava salt (see Tip)

2 tbsp / 30 mL water

12 oysters (your preference)

3 tbsp / 45 mL cold-pressed canola oil

---

TIP

To be honest, the black lava salt — which is just sea salt mixed with activated charcoal to give it a deep ebony colour — is just for show in this recipe. If you don't have any or can't find it at a specialty grocer or online, any coarse salt is a good option.

# KUSSHI OYSTERS WITH GRILLED ONION CREAM

MAKES 2 TO 3 SERVINGS (AS AN APPETIZER) | SPECIAL EQUIPMENT: OYSTER KNIFE

I was chef at an oyster bar for about a year. In that time, I shucked and ate *a lot* of oysters.

The Kusshi oyster, which is smaller, softer, and milder in flavour than some other types of oysters, tends to be everyone's favourite, especially for eating raw. Kusshi oysters are so delicate and light, and the onion cream in the recipe complements their inherent mild and sweet flavour. I enjoy them, too, but I also love brinier, more minerally oysters from the Atlantic. If you can't get Kusshis, use whichever oyster is freshest on the day you visit your seafood purveyor.

1    Preheat the grill to medium-high (400°F / 200°C).

2    Brush the hot grill with canola oil. Grill the white onion wedges and green onions until they take on dark char marks. Transfer the grilled white onion to a medium bowl. Set aside the grilled green onions.

3    To the bowl of grilled white onion, add the cream and ½ cup / 125 mL of chicken broth. Stir well and set aside for 1 hour to soak.

4    Remove and discard the grilled white onion. To the cream mixture, add the honey, 2 tbsp / 15 mL of the chopped chives, and the salt. Set aside.

5    Roughly chop the grilled green onions and transfer them to a blender. Add the olive oil, the remaining 2 tbsp / 30 mL of chicken broth, and the water. Blend on medium speed until combined, then increase the speed to high and blend until smooth.

6    Coat the bottom of a plate or shallow bowl with the grilled onion cream. Remove the oysters from their shells and arrange them evenly in the cream. Drizzle the oysters with the grilled green onion purée. Garnish the perimeter of the bowl with the remaining fresh chives and baby watercress. Place one potato chip on top of each oyster. Serve immediately.

Canola oil, for grilling

½ medium white onion, cut into ½-inch / 1-cm wedges

8 to 10 green onions (1 bundle), ends trimmed

1 cup / 250 mL whipping (35%) cream

½ cup / 125 mL + 2 tbsp / 30 mL good-quality chicken broth, divided

1 tbsp / 15 mL good-quality organic honey

¼ cup / 60 mL finely chopped fresh chives, divided

Pinch of salt

¾ cup / 175 mL olive oil

2 tbsp / 30 mL water

12 Kusshi oysters

1 small bunch baby watercress, for garnish

12 plain salted potato chips

# OYSTERS

Oysters are an endless world of interest for me. They're one of those foods where the more you learn, the less you realize you really know.

Always purchase oysters from a reputable seafood shop — they will select the best oysters for you at the time of purchase. West Coast oysters will keep in their shells in the fridge for up to 1 week when they are really fresh, and East Coast oysters in their shells for 2 weeks, if you store them in a crisper drawer between wet cloths (not on ice or in water).

Oysters should be alive when you are ready to shuck and eat them. Discard any with broken shells or that are open and do not close quickly when you handle them.

Shucking takes practice: Hold the oyster in your hand, with the deeper cup side of the shell down, with a clean cloth between the oyster and your palm. Holding the oyster knife in your other (dominant) hand, work the point of the knife into the joint or hinge where the two shells come together. Keep working the point in by moving it back and forth as you apply pressure to the hinge. When you feel you've got enough purchase with the tip of the knife in the hinge, twist it until you hear and feel the hinge "pop." Insert the knife into the oyster along the top shell and cut the oyster free of its attachment to the top shell. Lift off the top shell. The raw oyster should smell clean and "of the ocean." Make sure the oyster is free of any bits of shell that might have broken off as you opened it.

Shuck raw oysters just before you plan on eating them.

# CHILLED MUSSELS WITH STIFF CREAM AND SPRUCE TIPS

MAKES 4 TO 6 SERVINGS (AS AN APPETIZER)

Spruce tips are one of the easiest wild foods to forage, as spruce trees grow wild across Canada (see sidebar on page 38). From May to early June, soft light-green buds emerge from their brown papery casings (remove any casings before eating). The tips have a citrusy, resinous, grassy forest flavour that adds freshness to dishes like cold mussels. If you don't have access to spruce tips, substitute fresh dill, basil, or even diced green onions.

You can prepare this dish ahead of time and keep it chilled until you're ready to serve it. It makes a great finger food / appetizer.

1   Place the mussels in a colander in the sink and rinse well under cold running water. Scrub away any debris or barnacles that might be sticking to the shells. These days most mussels have already had the "beards" (fibrous strings that they grow) removed, but if necessary, carefully pull them off and cut as close to the shell as possible. Discard any mussels with broken shells, and any that are open and don't close when gently tapped.

2   In a large pot, bring the broth and garlic to a boil over medium high heat. Add the cleaned mussels, cover tightly with a lid, and cook just until the shells start to open, 3 to 4 minutes. Remove the pan from the heat immediately and discard any mussels that did not open. Cool, uncovered.

3   In a mixing bowl large enough to accommodate the mussels, combine ¼ cup / 60 mL of the spruce tips and the oil, dill, and salt and pepper. Gently toss to coat the mussels. Cover and refrigerate until ready to serve.

4   In a small saucepan, gently warm the cream cheese until it's quite soft. >>

2.2 lbs / 1 kg mussels

1 cup / 250 mL Pheasant Broth (recipe page 280) or good quality chicken broth

1 tbsp / 15 mL minced garlic

½ cup / 125 mL fresh spruce tips (see sidebar on page 38), divided

¼ cup / 60 mL cold-pressed canola oil

1½ cups / 375 mL finely chopped fresh dill

Pinch each of salt and freshly ground black pepper, or more to taste

2 cups / 500 mL full-fat cream cheese

½ cup / 125 mL whipping (35%) cream

1 rib celery, leaves trimmed and thinly shaved

5   Meanwhile, using a mortar and pestle, lightly bruise and smash the remaining ¼ cup / 60 mL of the spruce needles. Set aside.

6   Using a stand or electric mixer, whip the cream to stiff peaks. Gently fold in the softened cream cheese and the bruised spruce tips. Season to taste with salt and pepper.

7   Smear the whipped cream mixture in a thick stripe on a platter. Insert the hinges of the mussel shells firmly into the cream, positioning them at an angle. Garnish with the shaved celery.

8   To eat, scoop a little of the cream into the shell with the mussel meat.

**SPRUCE TIPS** are high in vitamin C and have antibacterial, antifungal, antimicrobial, and disinfectant properties, which makes them a medicine as well as a food. Harvest spruce tips in wilderness areas away from urban (or any) pollution during the spring. Remove the paper casings and make sure the tips are free of any other debris.

To prepare the spruce tips for this recipe, separate the needles from the tips, being careful to remove all of the wood, so that only the soft needles remain. Freeze the tips in a resealable freezer bag or container. You'll save on freezer space if you separate the greens from the wood of the tip.

# MY HOME NATION AND TERRITORY

**I AM FROM THE ENOCH CREE NATION.** The Elders tell us that before our Nation became associated with Chief Enoch Lapotac, we referred to ourselves by where we lived — our place name — *maskêkosihk* (muss-KAY-go-seehk), which literally means "at Little Muskeg."

The word *maskêk* ("muskeg") is similar to *maskihkiy*, meaning medicine. So we also consider ourselves people who live at the land of medicine. But more literally, we are the *maskêkosak* (muss-KAY-go-suk), "The Little Muskegs."

I live in Edmonton, but my restaurant, SC, is at the River Cree Resort & Casino on *maskêkosak* land in Treaty 6 Territory. The territory was established in 1876 as part of an agreement between the Indigenous leaders of what is now central Alberta and Saskatchewan and agents for the British Crown.

There are various dialects of the Cree language in Canada: Woods Cree, Swampy Cree, Moose Cree, Atikamekw Cree, and Plains Cree. Cree is spoken in Alberta, Saskatchewan, Manitoba, and across the border in Montana. The *maskêkosak* are among those who speak *nêhiyawêwin*, the Plains Cree language.

The *maskêkosak* include the colour white in the Medicine Wheel. Among other things, for us it represents white people — we know we can't get to where we're going alone. We shouldn't get there alone.

*tawâw: Progressive Indigenous Cuisine* is community-based. It's about my relationships with my community of chefs, even with chefs I've never met but who have influenced my cooking. It's about how I've created new connections with other Nations, from the Haida to the Kainai, from the Siksika to the Syilx. And it's a combination of experiences and influences, from the people who inspire me to those who celebrate with me and those who are always beside me.

Teepees set up for the annual Enoch Pow Wow.

# SCALLOPS WITH TORCHED GRAPEFRUIT AND WATERCRESS SAUCE

MAKES 2 TO 3 SERVINGS (AS AN APPETIZER) | SPECIAL EQUIPMENT: HAND TORCH (OPTIONAL)

Watercress (*Nasturtium officiale*) is one of those incredibly delicious wild foods that grows abundantly in streams, rivers, and marshes all over Canada. The stems are hollow, which helps the plants stay afloat as they form thick, green leafy mats. Later in the season, their flavour becomes spicier as they produce clusters of small white flowers. Cooking dampens the delicate peppery flavour of watercress, so don't overcook it in this — or any — recipe.

1   *Make the sauce:* Heat the oil in a small saucepan over medium heat. Add the butter, broth, shallot, garlic, and all but 5 sprigs of the watercress. Sauté for about 5 minutes or just until the watercress is wilted. Transfer the mixture to a blender and purée until smooth. Season with salt and pepper. Set aside to cool.

2   *Prepare the grapefruit:* Trim the top and bottom from the grapefruit and set it cut-side up so it is sitting flat on your work surface. Using a sharp paring knife, gently cut downward between the rind and inner fruit to remove the peel in long strips. Slice into the grapefruit lengthwise along the membranes and remove each segment (these are called "supremes"). You should end up with at least 6 pieces, but you'll need one piece for each scallop, so divide any larger pieces so that you have enough.

### FOR THE WATERCRESS SAUCE

1 tbsp / 15 mL canola or olive oil

¼ cup / 60 mL butter

¼ cup / 60 mL Pheasant Broth (recipe page 280) or good-quality chicken broth

1 small shallot, finely diced

2 cloves garlic, crushed

2 to 3 bunches watercress (about 4 cups / 1 L tightly packed leaves and stems, roots trimmed)

Salt and freshly ground black pepper, to taste

### FOR THE SCALLOPS

1 grapefruit

1 to 2 tbsp / 15 to 30 mL canola oil

6 to 10 medium fresh scallops, patted dry

Salt and freshly ground black pepper, to taste

1 tsp / 5 mL icing sugar

1 English cucumber, for garnish

3   *Cook the scallops:* Heat the oil in a heavy nonstick skillet over medium-high heat. Season the scallops with salt and pepper, then place carefully in the pan. (Watch out: The hot oil may spit. If it does, pull the pan off the heat until it calms down.) Sear the scallops for 3 minutes on each side, until they have a nice bronze crust. Reduce the heat to low and cook for another minute or two, until the scallops are just firm to touch (be careful not to overcook them). Divide the scallops evenly among your serving dishes.

4   *Assemble the dish:* Place a grapefruit segment on top of each scallop. Dust the top of each grapefruit segment with icing sugar (a small wire-mesh sieve works well). Caramelize the sugar with a hand torch (if using). If you don't have a hand torch, you can use the broiler of your oven: Set your broiler to medium heat (if you can), put the scallops on a baking sheet with the grapefruit segment and icing sugar, and broil until caramelized, watching carefully so as not to burn them. Remove from the oven as soon as the sugar melts and begins to turn brown.

5   Using a vegetable peeler, shave the cucumber into long thin ribbons. Twirl the strips around your finger to make a rose-like garnish.

6   Pour a generous amount of watercress sauce on a large serving plate. Arrange the scallops in the sauce (don't let the grapefruit fall off!). Garnish with the curls of cucumber and a few tendrils of fresh watercress. Serve immediately.

TIP

Watercress sauce is delicious on seafood but works equally well on red meats and chicken, too.

# FRIED SMELTS WITH WILD RICE, CARROTS, AND WILD LEEKS

MAKES 4 TO 6 SERVINGS

We all should be eating lower on the food chain, especially when it comes to fish. Smelts live in coastal seas and lakes, and run in streams in Canada. They can be caught in the spring via dip netting as they make their way to their spawning grounds or in the winter via ice fishing.

This dish is inspired by the eulachon fish (also known as the oolichan, ooligan, hooligan, and candlefish) of the West Coast, which is a smelt from the Pacific, harvested in Alaska down to the top of California. Eulachon is a very fatty fish that is caught and rendered for its grease by West Coast First Nations — hence the name "candlefish." It's also an important food source. Fresh smelt season on Canada's West Coast is April through October.

You can substitute whole anchovies (which are small, so maybe bump up the quantity), sardines, or herring for the smelts, if you like.

¾ cup / 175 mL water

¼ cup / 60 mL wild rice, rinsed and drained

1 bay leaf (fresh or dried)

1 medium carrot, peeled

4 cups + 2 tbsp / 1 L + 30 mL canola oil, divided

6 wild leeks (aka ramps), white-green or purple-green parts only (see sidebar on page 46), cut into 3-inch / 7.5-cm lengths

1 tbsp / 15 mL minced garlic

Fleur de sel, to taste

1 cup / 250 mL all-purpose flour

3 tbsp / 45 mL sea salt

1 tbsp / 15 mL freshly ground black pepper

1 tbsp / 15 mL red pepper flakes

8 whole smelts, cleaned and gutted

1 tsp / 5 mL bee pollen (see page 94)

4 sprigs fresh parsley, leaves only, roughly chopped

1   In a small pot, combine the water, the wild rice, a pinch of salt, and the bay leaf. Bring to a boil over medium-high heat. When it comes to a boil, stir well, reduce the heat to a simmer, cover with a lid, and cook until the rice opens up, 45 minutes. Drain any excess liquid and set aside.

2   Meanwhile, cut the carrot into ¼-inch / 0.5-cm coins and place in a pot with just enough water to cover. Season with a pinch of salt. Cook over medium heat until tender, about 7 minutes. Drain, transfer to a plate, and let cool slightly. >>

3    Heat 2 tbsp / 30 mL of the canola oil in a skillet over medium heat. Add the sliced carrots, cooked
     wild rice (along with the bay leaf), wild leeks, and garlic. Sauté until the leeks and garlic are
     fragrant and tender, 8 to 10 minutes. Season to taste with salt.

4    In a bowl, combine the flour, sea salt, pepper, and red pepper flakes. Dredge the smelts in the
     seasoned flour, making sure to get it into the cavities as well.

5    In a heavy, deep pot over medium-high heat, bring the 4 cups / 1 L of oil up to 325°F / 170°C.
     Carefully add the floured smelts to the hot oil one or two at a time. Cook, turning occasionally,
     until their skin is golden brown and the smelts are very firm (the cook time will depend on the
     size of the smelts; check the inside belly of the fish to see if it is fully cooked). Remove the fried
     smelts from the oil using a wire-mesh scoop, tapping it once or twice to remove any excess oil,
     and place on a wire rack or paper-towel-lined platter. Set aside.

6    Spread the carrot, wild rice, and leek medley over a wooden cutting board or serving platter, or
     divide evenly among individual dishes. Carefully arrange the smelts on top. Sprinkle with the bee
     pollen, parsley, and fleur de sel. Serve immediately.

WILD LEEK (*Allium tricoccum*) is also known as ramps, wild onion, and wild garlic.
It tastes somewhere between onion and garlic. They're only in season for a few weeks in
the spring. When foraging, it's very important not to over-harvest them because they
reproduce slowly. In fact, responsible harvesters leave enough in the ground (i.e., the
bulb and some of the stems/leaves) to keep wild crops intact for seasons to come.
(Note: This recipe only calls for the portion of the wild leek that grows above ground.)
Please forage responsibly!

# SMOKED HAIDA GWAII SABLEFISH WITH CUCUMBERS, SPROUTED BEANS, AND ROSEHIPS

MAKES 2 TO 4 SERVINGS | SPECIAL EQUIPMENT: DEBONING TWEEZERS

This is similar to a "shore lunch," something you'd put together on a fishing trip using whatever wild foods — dandelions and wild rosehips — you could gather and cook quickly over an open fire.

Sablefish (also known as black cod) is buttery and rich, and comes from the pristine Northern Pacific ocean waters around Haida Gwaii, home to the Haida nation. They have been managing the fishery and living off the ocean abundance for over 13,000 years. There's an excellent company on Canada's West Coast called Haida Wild. I buy my sablefish already cold-smoked and packaged in a handy fillet from them.

Sablefish is an incredible treasure, but apparently in North America we export over 70 percent of it to Japan. That's okay. It's a sustainably managed fish, so we likely have time to catch on to what our Japanese friends already know.

1   Preheat the grill to medium-high (400°F / 200°C).

2   Using deboning tweezers, pick out any remaining bones from the fillet. There's also a central bone running from the collar (neck) halfway to the tail. Take a sharp paring knife and cut around and underneath this bone to remove it. Then, using a long, sharp knife, carefully cut between the flesh and the skin, peeling the skin back as you go. Cut the sablefish into bite-size pieces, about 2-inch / 5-cm squares.

3   Place the dandelion greens on the dry grill just until they start to wilt and turn black around the edges and points of the leaves. Transfer them to a bowl and toss them with the lemon oil.

4   To serve, arrange the grilled dandelion greens on a platter. Scatter the cucumber slices, sprouted beans, and rosehips over the greens. Place the smoked sablefish on top and season with salt and pepper.

1 fillet cold-smoked sablefish

10 to 12 long dandelion leaves

¼ cup / 60 mL lemon oil (see sidebar, opposite)

½ English cucumber, cut into ⅛-inch / 3-mm coins

1 cup / 250 mL assorted sprouted bean mix (see Tip)

½ cup / 125 mL dried rosehips

Salt and freshly ground black pepper, to taste

---

**TIP**

You can find assorted sprouted bean mix at most grocery stores.

---

**YOU CAN PURCHASE LEMON OIL,** which is oil infused with lemon rind, at gourmet food stores. You can also make it at home: Using a Y-peeler, remove long but shallow strips of rind from 2 lemons (avoid the white pith). Put the rinds in a sterilized 1 cup / 250 mL glass canning jar. (Sterilize by boiling the jar and the lid in water for a few minutes.) Pour about ¾ cup / 185 mL of very mild-tasting oil (canola or a mild olive oil) over the rinds. Seal the jar and refrigerate for up to 4 days to infuse the oil. After 4 days, remove the peel with very clean tweezers and discard. The oil is now ready for use. It will keep, covered and refrigerated, for a week.

# YELLOWFIN TUNA WITH SEAWEED SALAD AND GLASS NOODLES

MAKES 4 SERVINGS

You may be surprised to find a Japanese-inspired dish in a contemporary Indigenous cookbook, but I've had a long-running fascination and love for Japanese cuisine. I go for it over French and European food almost every time. I love the precision of Japanese food, and how clearly it represents itself as a cooking philosophy. It proves to me over and over again that you don't need to start with a classic French mindset or flavour base, and it inspires me when dreaming up Indigenous dishes. It also reminds me that in my lifetime Canadians of all backgrounds have come to love Japanese cooking. Someday the same will be said for Indigenous cuisine.

### FOR THE SEAWEED SALAD

3 oz / 85 g glass noodles (also known as cellophane noodles)

½ oz / 15 g dried wakame or kombu (kelp) seaweed

3 tbsp / 45 mL unseasoned rice vinegar

3 tbsp / 45 mL Japanese tamari or soy sauce

1 tbsp / 15 mL sesame oil

2 tsp / 10 mL good-quality organic honey (see page 134) or granulated sugar

½ tsp / 2.5 mL red pepper flakes

1 tbsp / 15 mL grated peeled fresh gingerroot

½ tsp / 2.5 mL minced garlic

2 tbsp + 2 tsp / 30 mL + 10 mL sesame seeds (white or black), divided

Sea salt

Juice of ½ lime

### FOR THE SESAME MAYO SAUCE

¾ cup / 175 mL mayonnaise

2 tbsp / 30 mL sesame oil

1 tbsp / 15 mL hoisin sauce

1 tbsp / 15 mL Sriracha sauce or Gochujang (Korean chili paste)

3 tbsp / 45 mL toasted sesame seeds

½ tsp / 2.5 mL ground cumin

15 fresh chives

Salt and freshly ground black pepper

### FOR THE TUNA

3 sheets green nori

Pinch of sea salt

1 yellowfin tuna loin, sliced across the grain into 12 pieces (½ inch / 1 cm thick)

2 tbsp / 30 mL canola oil

1 tbsp / 15 mL togarashi seasoning or red pepper flakes

1   *Make the salad:* To cook the glass noodles, place them in a large heatproof bowl and cover completely in boiling water. Cover the bowl with plastic wrap or a tight-fitting lid and set aside for 10 to 15 minutes, until tender but firm.

2   Meanwhile, place the seaweed in a large bowl with lots of cold water. Let soak for about 5 minutes, or until the leaves are very flexible. Drain well (reserve bowl) and cut the prepared seaweed into very thin strips. Return to the reserved bowl and set aside.

3   In a small bowl, whisk together the unseasoned rice vinegar, tamari, sesame oil, honey, red pepper flakes, grated ginger, and minced garlic. Set aside.

4   Once the noodles are ready, rinse them under cold running water until completely chilled. Drain well and place them in the bowl with the seaweed. Add 2 tsp / 10 mL of the sesame seeds and the vinegar mixture. Season with a pinch of salt and a squeeze of lime. Toss well to combine. Taste and add more salt, if needed. Set aside.

5   *Make the sauce:* In a blender, combine the mayonnaise, sesame oil, hoisin sauce, Sriracha or Gochujang, sesame seeds, cumin, chives, and salt and pepper. Blend until smooth. Set aside.

6   *Prepare the tuna:* In a food processor, combine the nori sheets, remaining 2 tbsp / 30 mL sesame seeds, and a pinch of salt. Pulse until you achieve a coarse texture, like coffee grounds. Transfer all but 2 tbsp / 30 mL of the sesame-nori mixture to a shallow bowl or pie plate. Roll the tuna loin in the sesame-nori mixture to coat, pressing it firmly onto the surface. (You can also roll the coated loin in plastic wrap very tightly, give it a good squeeze, and then unwrap it.)

7   In a cast-iron skillet, heat the oil over medium-high heat until it shimmers. Sear the tuna loin by just lightly touching each side to the hot pan (you are not trying to fully cook the tuna, just the top ¼ inch / 0.5 cm on each side). Let the seared tuna rest on a cutting board for a minute or so. Using a sharp knife, cut the tuna across the grain into twelve ½-inch / 1-cm pieces.

8   To serve, put ⅓ cup / 80 mL of the sesame cream sauce in each serving bowl. Top with about ⅓ cup / 80 mL of the seaweed salad. Lay 3 pieces of tuna across the salad. Sprinkle with a pinch of togarashi seasoning and a pinch of the reserved nori sesame crumble.

# RABBIT IN A GARDEN

MAKES 2 SERVINGS

We hunted rabbits on our acreage when I was young. Mom also grew a huge garden. That's where the two main inspirations for this dish came from. Also, Central Alberta is farming country, where bright-yellow canola fields run for miles and saskatoon bushes bend with berry clusters in the woodlands.

Rabbit meat is extremely lean. As long as you don't overcook the legs, they'll be delicious.

## FOR THE RABBIT

4 to 6 cremini mushrooms,
    roughly chopped

6 tbsp / 90 mL canola oil, divided

1 tbsp / 15 mL minced garlic

2 rabbit legs

Pinch each of salt and freshly ground
    black pepper

½ cup / 125 mL rubbed sage (see Tip)

## FOR THE GARDEN

5 large kale leaves

Pinch of fleur de sel

2 cups / 500 mL canola oil, or more as
    needed to shallow-fry

3 cremini mushrooms

2 radishes, including the tops

½ cup / 125 mL fennel tops and fronds
    (approx.)

1 English cucumber, for garnish

## FOR THE SASKATOON BERRY VINAIGRETTE

½ cup / 125 mL cold-pressed canola oil

Juice of 1 lime

¼ cup / 60 mL pomegranate syrup

2 tbsp / 30 mL water

Salt and freshly ground black pepper,
    to taste

¼ cup / 60 mL saskatoon berries or
    mossberries (see sidebar on page 58)

---

**TIP**

Ground sage is made by grinding the entire sage leaf to a powder. It loses its vibrant flavour very quickly, and I find that it eventually takes on an unpleasant musty or stale quality. Rubbed sage — literally the rubbings of sage leaves only — has an incredibly lovely, truer-to-fresh-sage flavour that will stay bright for 6 months when stored in a cool, dry, dark place.

1   In a small bowl, combine the chopped mushrooms, 2 tbsp / 30 mL of the oil, and the garlic. Set aside.

2   Preheat the oven to 350°F / 180°C (see Tip on page 57).

3   *Prepare the rabbit:* Place the rabbit on a cutting board. Using a sharp knife, remove the large upper bone from both thighs but leave the smaller bone in each leg; set the legs aside. Lay the thighs flat, then cut horizontally through the meat until it is almost cut in half (butterflied) to make a pocket for the stuffing. Season the cavity with salt and pepper. Divide the mushroom mix evenly between the thighs and then roll them closed. Using butcher's twine, truss the legs shut.

4   Spread the rubbed sage over a plate. Roll the legs in the rubbed sage until evenly covered.

5   In a heavy skillet, heat ¼ cup / 60 mL of the oil over high heat until it shimmers. Sear the legs on each side for 2 minutes, or until you get a nice golden-brown crust on the flat parts of the meat. Transfer the seared legs to a dry pan and roast in the preheated oven for 12 to 15 minutes, until the internal temperature of each leg reaches 160°F / 71°C. Remove the pan from the oven and set aside to let the meat rest.

6   *Deep-fry the kale leaves:* Fill a deep pot with about 3 inches / 7.5 cm of oil and heat to 350°F / 180°C (you'll know it's hot enough when you see little "rivers" appear along the bottom of the pot). Fry 3 of the kale leaves until golden brown. Using a wire-mesh scoop or slotted spoon, transfer the fried leaves to paper towel to drain. Season with a pinch of fleur de sel. Set aside.

7   *Prepare the "garden":* Using a rolling pin, flatten out the remaining 2 kale leaves until tender. Using a paring knife, cut the centre stems out and discard. Rip the leaves into bite-size pieces with your fingers. Cut the mushrooms lengthwise into ¼-inch / 0.5-cm pieces. Tear the radish tops into bite-size pieces. Trim the tops and bottoms from both radishes; peel one and cut it in half. Thinly slice the unpeeled radish into ⅛-inch / 3-mm coins. Roughly chop the fennel tops and fronds. Using a vegetable peeler, shave 5 or 6 long strips from the cucumber. Roll them around your little finger to make a rose garnish, and set aside.

8   *Make the vinaigrette:* In a small bowl, whisk together the cold-pressed oil, lime juice, pomegranate syrup, and water. Season with salt and pepper to taste. Add the saskatoons and stir until coated.

9   *Assemble the dish:* Combine the raw kale leaves, mushrooms, radish coins and tops, and fennel in a mixing bowl. Add the vinaigrette and gently toss (you don't want to crush the saskatoons or break the mushroom slices).

10  Arrange one and a half fried kale leaves on the bottom of each serving plate. Cut a ¾-inch / 2-cm round slice from the end of each rabbit thigh. Place one piece, cut-side up, on each of the plates. Place one leg, bone facing up, on each plate. Arrange the dressed salad around the rabbit, dividing it equally. Place half of a peeled radish on each plate. Finish by garnishing each plate with curls of cucumber. Serve immediately.

**RABBIT** is an excellent animal on which to hone your home butchering skills. It's small enough that it's easy to handle, and you're not on the hook for a huge amount of meat when you're done. There are excellent resources on the internet to show you how to break down a rabbit and debone the legs. Save the breast and other meat for a stew with nice big chunks of lardons (cubes of fatty bacon).

---
TIP

If you are using a conventional oven, you may need to either cook the dish a little longer or increase the oven temperature by 25°F / 4°C.

---

## SASKATOON BERRIES

Found in abundance in Alberta, Saskatchewan, and into Manitoba, saskatoon berries (*Amelanchier alnifolia*) are also known as serviceberries, shadbush berries, and juneberries. It is also possible to find varietals and lesser-known relatives as far north as the Yukon and Northwest Territories, and as far south as the northern plains of the United States. Saskatoon bushes, which are rather spindly and willow-like, produce clusters of small, white blooms in early spring. In southern parts of Canada in mid-June and elsewhere during July and August, the fruit ripen in small masses of 6 to 12 bluish-purple berries. Less sweet but similar in flavour to blueberries, saskatoons also have a distinctive marzipan/almond taste. They are a treat eaten fresh, out of hand, in mid-summer or when made into jams or syrups for pancakes, or baked into saskatoon berry pies.

# LAMB CHOPS WITH BEETS

MAKES 4 TO 5 SERVINGS (16 CHOPS) | SPECIAL EQUIPMENT: RUBBER OR LATEX GLOVES (OPTIONAL)

I really like making meals that don't require the use of utensils to enjoy them. So while I am not a huge fan of strong lamb flavours, I do love lamb chops. They have built-in handles: You can just pick one up, mop up some beet sauce, and enjoy.

1 In a large pot, bring the bison broth to a vigorous boil over high heat. Reduce the heat to medium and simmer, uncovered, for about 45 minutes to an hour, until it reduces to a syrup (watch it carefully to avoid scorching). You should end up with about 6 tbsp / 90 mL of reduced broth.

2 Meanwhile, cook the beets in a pot of boiling water for 30 to 45 minutes (depending on the size of the beets), until they pierce easily through to the centre with a paring knife. Drain and let cool slightly. When they're cool enough to handle, slip off the skins (you may want to wear rubber or latex gloves to avoid staining your hands).

3 Place 2 medium cooked beets in a blender. Add the maple syrup and reduced broth. Purée until smooth. Taste and season with salt, about ¼ tsp / 1 mL or to taste. Set aside. Cut the remaining beets into ½-inch / 1-cm cubes and set aside.

4 Preheat the oven to 350°F / 180°C (see Tip).

5 Meanwhile, season the racks of lamb with salt and pepper, to taste. Heat a cast iron skillet over high heat. Add 1 tbsp / 15 mL of oil and sear the lamb, browning on both sides of each rack, for about 3 minutes total per rack. >>

8 cups / 2 L Bison Bone Broth (recipe page 276)

8 medium red and yellow beets, leaves trimmed

¼ cup / 60 mL pure maple syrup

Salt and freshly ground black pepper, to taste

2 racks of lamb, with about 8 lamb chops each

2 tbsp / 30 mL canola oil, divided

1 small leek, white and pale green parts only, cut into ¼-in / 0.5-cm rounds

12 fresh mint leaves, for garnish

12 blackberries, for garnish

---
**TIP**

If you are using a conventional oven, you may need to either cook the dish a little longer or increase the oven temperature by 25°F / 4°C.

---

>>

6   Transfer the seared lamb to a wire rack in a roaster.
Roast in the preheated oven until the internal
temperature reaches 125°F / 52°C (for rare), about
10 minutes (depending on the size of the racks), or
a few minutes longer to 135°F / 57°C (for medium-
rare). Remove from the oven and tent very loosely
with aluminum foil. Let rest for 5 minutes.

7   While the lamb is cooking, add the remaining oil
to a skillet over medium heat. Heat the oil until it
shimmers, then add the sliced leeks. Sauté the leeks
on one side only for about 5 minutes, until golden.

8   To serve, cut the cooked racks into individual chops.
Place a dollop of beet purée onto each plate. Arrange
3 or 4 chops per plate (depending on how many
people you are serving), along with some of the
caramelized leeks and a few cubes of cooked beets.
Garnish with mint leaves and fresh berries.

# PORK CHOPS WITH QUICK-PICKLED ONIONS, GARLIC AIOLI, AND A DOLLOP OF BISON "RAGÙ"

MAKES 4 SERVINGS

Pork chops are comfort food. When I was a kid, pork chops cooked in mushroom soup was a food craze. (My dad also used to love eating Spam, that salty canned, jellied pork — it was a generational thing.) This dish is meant to bring back fond memories of home but without the highly processed canned foods. To simplify this dish, you can omit the garlic purée and the bison "ragù," if you like.

### FOR THE GARLIC AIOLI

2 large egg yolks, at room temperature

1 tsp / 5 mL freshly squeezed lemon juice

½ tsp / 2.5 mL Tabasco sauce

½ cup / 125 mL canola or extra virgin olive oil

1 tbsp / 15 mL minced garlic (about 3 medium cloves) or garlic purée (see page 209)

1 tbsp / 15 mL chopped fresh parsley

½ tsp / 2.5 mL each salt and freshly ground black pepper

### FOR THE PICKLED ONIONS

1 cup / 250 mL water

1 cup / 250 mL white vinegar

¼ cup / 60 mL granulated sugar

2 tbsp / 30 mL kosher salt

1 large red onion

### FOR THE PORK CHOPS

1 tbsp / 15 mL butter

1 tbsp / 15 mL canola oil

4 centre-cut pork chops (1 inch / 2.5 cm thick)

Salt and freshly ground black pepper, to taste

¼ cup / 60 mL finely chopped fresh parsley leaves (curly or flat-leaf)

¼ cup / 60 mL garlic purée (see page 209)

½ cup / 125 mL Bison "Ragù" (recipe page 255)

1   *Make the aioli:* Whisk together the egg yolks, lemon juice, and Tabasco in a bowl. While whisking, very gradually, drops at a time, add the oil. Whisk until the mixture has thickened and emulsified. Add the garlic, parsley, and salt and pepper and whisk well (the finished aioli should have the consistency of mayonnaise).

2   *Make the pickled onions:* Combine the water, white vinegar, sugar, and salt in a pot. Cook over medium heat, stirring occasionally, until the sugar and salt are completely dissolved, about 5 minutes.

3   Using a mandoline or a sharp knife, slice the onion very thinly. Transfer the sliced onions to a heatproof container. Pour the hot brine over top. Set aside for about 15 minutes. Once cooled completely, they are ready.

4   *Prepare the pork chops:* Place the butter and oil in a cast iron pan over high heat. Season the pork chops with salt and pepper. When the oil mixture shimmers, brown the pork chops for a minute or two on each side to get a nice golden crust. Reduce the heat to medium and continue cooking the pork chops, turning occasionally, until they reach an internal temperature of 155°F / 68°C. Transfer the cooked chops to a tray, tent with aluminum foil, and let rest for 5 to 7 minutes. Garnish with finely chopped parsley.

5   *Assemble the dish:* Smear a heaping tablespoon of garlic purée on each plate. Place a pork chop at the thick end of the smear. Add 1 tbsp / 15 mL garlic aioli near each pork chop, along with 2 tbsp / 30 mL warm bison ragù and 2 tbsp / 30 mL pickled red onions. Serve immediately.

# CHOPPED BISON WITH NETTLE PESTO ON RYE TOAST

MAKES 4 TO 8 SERVINGS

This is my take on spring steak tartare, using bison. I've included hemp oil for its intense green grassy colour and flavour reminiscent of native Prairie grasses, which is what bison graze on. Then there's the green of the nettle, springtime's ultimate superfood! Sunflower is also an important crop that farmers domesticated thousands of years ago.

Make a batch of this nettle pesto (add some Parmesan cheese) to toss with cooked pasta or spaghetti squash. It also makes a great addition to a bowl of potato soup or poached whitefish — just add a dollop before serving.

### FOR THE NETTLE PESTO

2 cups / 500 mL loosely packed stinging nettles, leaves only (see page 25)

½ cup / 125 mL hemp oil or any high-quality cold-pressed oil (canola, flax, extra virgin olive)

2 tbsp / 30 mL minced garlic

3 tbsp / 45 mL roasted salted sunflower seeds

¼ cup / 60 mL water

1 tsp / 5 mL salt

½ tsp / 2.5 mL freshly ground black pepper

### FOR THE CHOPPED BISON

1 × 1-lb / 450-g eye of bison (a great substitute for tenderloin), finely diced

1 tsp / 5 mL kosher salt

¾ tsp / 3 mL freshly ground black pepper

### FOR SERVING

4 slices rye bread

½ cup / 125 mL cold-pressed flax, hemp, or canola oil

2 green onions, finely chopped

1  *Make the pesto:* Bring a large pot of water to a boil. Prepare an ice water bath (a large bowl filled with cold water and ice cubes). Carefully add the nettle leaves to the boiling water and cook for 1 to 3 minutes, just until the leaves wilt and turn bright green (the exact time will depend on the age and the thickness of the nettle leaves). Using a slotted spoon, quickly transfer the blanched nettles to the prepared ice bath and let sit for about 30 seconds. Using your hands, gently squeeze out any excess water and transfer to a blender. >>

2   To the blender, add the hemp oil, garlic, sunflower seeds, water, salt, and pepper. Purée until it reaches the consistency of hummus (if the paste is too stiff, add more water). Transfer to a resealable container and refrigerate for up to a week.

3   *Prepare the bison and assemble the dish:* Just before serving, toss the diced bison with the salt and pepper in a bowl. Add the pesto and stir well. Toast the bread and brush with the oil. Top the toast with scoopfuls of the bison and garnish with the green onions. Serve immediately.

---

**TIP**

The trick to making steak tartare is to source quality bison or beef from your specialty butcher. You want something fairly tender and lean — tenderloin is a great choice, but eye of round on a bison is also excellent and tends to be less expensive. You're chopping it up into small pieces, anyway. Keep the meat chilled until just before mincing, as it'll be firmer and easier to cut. Use a very sharp chef's knife and cut into about 1/8-inch / 3-mm dice for a fine tartare, or slightly larger dice for a chunkier style. Lastly, keep everything cold; tartare tastes better when slightly chilled.

# DEEP-FRIED BANNOCK WITH SASKATOON BERRIES AND BIRCH SYRUP

MAKES 4 SERVINGS | SPECIAL EQUIPMENT: DEEP-FRYER OR DEEP POT ON THE STOVE

I have a love–hate relationship with bannock (also known as fry bread) — see my explanation on page 287. It's a delicious and important food in Indigenous communities. At the end of the day, however, it's most beloved when deep-fried and drizzled with honey and sugar. Enjoy it, but only from time to time.

1   Make the bannock dough following the instructions in step one on page 286.

2   While the dough is resting, preheat a deep-fryer or fill a deep pot with about 3 inches / 7.5 cm of oil and heat to 350°F / 180°C.

3   With floured hands, divide the dough into 2-oz / 55-g portions — about the size of a large egg — and shape into ovals.

4   Using your thumb, poke two holes into each portion of dough and then gently drop the dough balls into the hot oil. Fry, flipping as necessary, until golden brown all over, about 2 minutes. Using a wire-mesh scoop or slotted spoon, transfer the fried dough to a plate lined in paper towel. Set aside.

5   Place the sugar in a shallow plate. Rinse the saskatoon berries under cold running water, drain, and then roll them in the sugar. (If using frozen berries, you can toss them directly into the sugar.)

6   To serve, cut each piece of bannock in half or quarters, drizzle with warm syrup or honey, and top with a spoonful of sweetened berries.

1 batch Bannock (recipe page 286)

Neutral-flavoured cooking oil (such as canola), for frying

¼ cup / 60 mL granulated sugar

2 cups / 500 mL saskatoon berries (fresh or frozen)

½ cup / 125 mL pure birch or maple syrup or good-quality organic honey (see page 134)

# HIGHBUSH CRANBERRY, MINT, AND MAPLE SIP

MAKES 4 SERVINGS | SPECIAL EQUIPMENT: DEEP-FRY THERMOMETER

Highbush cranberries grow abundantly in woodlands from British Columbia to Newfoundland. They are not "true" cranberries, though they resemble one another enough that you could swap regular cranberries for highbush. Highbush cranberries are a Viburnum, a member of the honeysuckle family. It's best to pick these berries in the dead of winter. Not only do they sweeten and lose some of their excessive tannins after freezing, but they are easier to spot in the woods when the bright-red berries are all that is left hanging on the willowy branches of the trees. Then they are a perfect spring tonic with maple syrup and fresh mint.

1   In a small saucepan over medium heat, cook the cranberries, mashing them gently with the back of a spoon, for about 5 minutes or until the skins have completely broken down. Using a fine-mesh sieve, strain the liquid into a bowl; discard the pulp and large pips.

2   Combine the strained cranberry juice, maple syrup, and mint leaves in a blender and blend until smooth.

3   In a small saucepan, heat the oil to 350°F / 180°C. Add the mint sprigs and fry until the leaves turn deep green and stop bubbling in the oil, about 2 minutes. Using a slotted spoon, transfer the fried mint to paper towel. While still hot, sprinkle the leaves with the sugar.

4   Divide the syrup evenly among 4 small tumbler glasses. To each glass, add ½ cup / 125 mL of water and garnish with a sprig of fried mint.

1 cup / 250 mL highbush cranberries, picked in winter and kept frozen

2 to 3 tbsp / 30 to 45 mL pure maple syrup, or to taste

4 to 6 fresh mint leaves

½ cup / 125 mL neutral-flavoured cooking oil (such as canola), for frying

4 sprigs fresh mint

1 tbsp / 15 mL granulated sugar

2 cups / 500 mL sparkling or still cold water

# COWBOY SMITHx

**COWBOY SMITHx** is one of the most charismatic people you'll ever meet. If he says five words to you, you will remember all five words. And no matter which five words he chooses, you know he knows his shit.

Cowboy is a Blackfoot filmmaker and artist from the Piikani and Kainai Nations on Treaty 7 territory located in Southern Alberta. He's also the founder and curator of REDx Talks. That's how I met him.

Everyone has heard of TED Talks, right? Well, REDx Talks is much cooler and more interesting. It's an international Indigenous speakers series that creates multimedia conversations on traditional Indigenous territories in the spirit of oral tradition. The presentations are themed around truth, reconciliation, and the future. REDx explores Indigenous issues and inclusive conversations beyond the Indigenous experience.

REDx is an acronym for Resilience, Empowerment, and Discourse. The silent X recognizes the treaties that were signed (often with an *X* by the Indigenous partners in the treaty). It's the unknown in mathematics, says Cowboy, and there's so much he doesn't know about his culture due to the colonial processes and intergenerational trauma of genocide. He also refers to the X as acknowledgement of the four directions, and of

the "knowledge bundle" that REDx Talks creates.

In 2016, the REDx Talks team approached me to cater their first REDx Talk on Treaty 6 territory in Edmonton. We had such great conversations right off the bat, I was invited to speak at the event. The name of that REDx event was "Art Is the Medicine," so my talk was "Food Is the Medicine."

I've learned a lot from Cowboy. He pushes me to develop my public speaking skills, and he's expanding my idea of the importance of food within our journeys in the Indigenous community. He also talks a lot about the "frequencies of the land"—how we connect to the land—which can only be translated by the people of the land. Indigenous peoples have been translating these frequencies for thousands of years. And you hear those frequencies through the drums, through the songs, through the language. You see them at the ceremonies. You taste them in the food.

It's such an interesting thought—that a baseline connection exists already, that it always has and always will. We just need to tune in, listen, and pay attention to what it's telling us so it can guide us. It's now something I think about when dreaming about cooking and creating new dishes. I am grateful that Cowboy was willing to share his thoughts for a few pages in this book.

# RECLAIMING THE CULINARY FREQUENCIES OF THE LAND

## BY COWBOY SMITHx

**WHAT I'VE BEEN ABLE** to do with my skills as a filmmaker and a storyteller is to reactivate oral tradition with REDx Talks and through REDx Talks. We were looking for someone to help with food for REDx Talks. Shane is a pioneer of the resurgence of Indigenous food. After one meeting, it was a no-brainer. We were going to work with this guy for the rest of time.

Ceremony and gathering, confluence, renewal, treaty, celebration—there is no ceremony without food. And with all the cultural genocide we've faced as Indigenous people, we need as many connections as possible, with all practices of art. Food has always been the centrepiece of Indigenous culture, and Shane has been activating people's connection to their culture through food.

Food is one area of Indigenous culture that needs to be decolonized the most because of how unhealthy many people's diets have become. And most of that—the lack of nutrition—has been due to a lack of resources. During the ration years with the Indian agents, spoiled meat would be deliberately delivered to communities and families. Mouldy rice and potatoes, too. Anything to push people to the brink. How do you heal from that? We need to reset everything.

Even bannock is problematic. Shane and I get in trouble for calling this out, but bannock, or fry bread, is not a natural part of our Indigenous diet. It's white flour and it's deep-fried. It's delicious as hell—don't get me wrong—but it's not from here. If you served fry bread to our ancestors, they probably would have blasted you with an arrow through the heart because they could see and sense that it's of a lower frequency. It's not healthy for you. Because of our genetic structures, we're missing certain enzymes to break down different types of sugars. That is why you see diabetes pandemics in our communities. We're still new to this type of diet.

And you know, for thousands of years, I guarantee you, we didn't have anyone with heart disease. We didn't have anyone with diabetes. We didn't have anyone dealing with cancer. Because we lived such a healthy lifestyle. All natural, free range, and organic—like the hipsters are doing now. That was our life for thousands of years. One of the greatest frequencies of the land that we're missing is the migration of the bison. We humans get caught up in our own self-importance and think we're the be-all and end-all. But there are four-legged creatures and airborne creatures—our brothers and our sisters, the animals of this earth—that we must share this territory with because in a lot of cases, they make the ultimate sacrifice, giving their bodies so that we can survive.

That's the bottom line. It may freak people out a bit, but it's the Indigenous foods that really carry the primary frequencies of this territory.

When you look at societal trends, it's really funny—how everyone is catching up with where our ancestors were thousands of years ago. As Dr. Leroy Little Bear says, we Indigenous people have been waiting in the wings long enough. We've had these answers for thousands of years. We've been marginalized and brushed aside—victims of systemic violence and racism for far too long. That type of entitlement catches up to you, and I sense these kinds of colonial constructs crumbling within the next 100 years.

In a lot of ways, I'm on the same journey as Shane. I was not raised in Indigenous cultures. I was raised Catholic, and as my name indicates, I was raised in a ranch-and-rodeo culture. My grandparents and my great-grandparents had to follow those rules, those new protocols of the Catholic church. They were literally beat into them. A big part of the disconnect comes from residential schools.

We're all victims of colonization, all of us, because non-Indigenous people have been robbed of this beautiful culture, these beautiful frequencies. We've all been shaken and shocked. We all have different levels of privilege and experience, and we need to fill the gaps for each other.

You build one side of an arc and, at some point, you're going to need that keystone. We're doing it through art, film, culinary arts, writing, poetry, and songs. And we will finally find our keystone. We'll finally get to a place where Indigenous people and newcomers to this territory will collectively coexist and build from the beginning, outward.

Through REDx Talks, Shane has the opportunity to reactivate the feast, the ceremonial keystone, the loadstone of the community. Ceremony and gathering is the feast.

*"We're all victims of colonization, all of us, because non-Indigenous people have been robbed of this beautiful culture, these beautiful frequencies."*

ᐤᣆ ∧ᑉ

*nîpin*

# SUMMER

# SUMMER

# SEASHORE SOUP

MAKES 4 TO 6 SERVINGS

I have family on the West Coast. When I was young, my parents would take us there to visit. I remember walking along the seashore and finding clamshells, fish bones, and skeletons — treasures to a child. This soup is based on those childhood memories.

1   Combine the oil and onion in a heavy-bottomed soup pot. Sauté over medium heat until the onion turns pale golden, 4 to 5 minutes. Add the carrot and celery, and sauté for another 5 minutes. Pour in the white wine, and add the bay leaf and thyme. Gently simmer until the liquid has reduced by about half.

2   Reduce the heat to low, add the saffron strands, and simmer for about 2 minutes. Stir in the clam nectar, water, and seafood base (if using). Bring back to a simmer. Add the potatoes and cook for about 20 minutes, until the potatoes are tender.

3   Add the haddock and salmon to the pot, along with the clams and mussels. Gently stir, and cook for about 5 minutes, until the fish has turned opaque and the mussels and clams have opened (discard any that remain closed). Taste and adjust the seasoning with salt and pepper, if needed. Serve immediately, garnished with chopped dill.

---

**TIP**

Seafood base paste is a concentrated form of seafood stock. You can find it at a good fish monger or even at well-stocked gourmet stores or specialty delis.

---

1 tbsp / 15 mL canola oil

⅔ cup / 160 mL diced onion

⅓ cup / 80 mL diced carrot

⅓ cup / 80 mL diced celery

⅓ cup / 80 mL dry white wine

1 bay leaf (dried)

2 sprigs fresh thyme

5 strands saffron

2 cups / 500 mL clam nectar

2 cups / 500 mL water

2 tbsp / 30 mL seafood base paste (optional; see Tip)

1 ⅓ cups / 330 mL diced potato (peeled or not, as you prefer)

1 × 6-oz / 170-g haddock fillet, skin off and pinboned, cut into bite-size pieces

1 × 6-oz / 170-g salmon fillet, skin off and pinboned, cut into bite-size pieces

12 clams, scrubbed

6 mussels, scrubbed and debearded

Salt and freshly ground black pepper, to taste

Chopped fresh dill fronds, for garnish

# SALMON PEMMICAN

MAKES 1 ROLL | SPECIAL EQUIPMENT: FOOD DEHYDRATOR; LARGE MORTAR AND PESTLE

Historically, pemmican was made with air-dried and pounded bison meat and included hard organ fat and berries. Ancestors knew that you needed to mix fat in with the very lean protein; otherwise, no matter how much of it you ate, you would die.

Pemmican is an acquired taste — or texture, really — but it's genius in terms of nutrition: with its dense caloric impact, protein, fat, and even carbohydrates (when dried berries are mixed in), it's the original survival food. It's also portable and has a long shelf life, though I suggest you store it in the fridge. For long-term storage, keep it in the freezer.

Even though I'm from the Prairies, where bison pemmican is more common, I like to make pemmican with dried and pounded salmon. I love the colour and the memories of the West Coast that salmon always evokes for me. However, this foundational recipe works well with other fish like arctic char and even freshwater lake fish like pickerel. You can experiment with other fish, too.

Note that this recipe does require two days of advance prep: a day of curing and then a day of dehydrating the fish or meat. Plan ahead. If you want to incorporate saskatoon berries, begin with about ½ cup / 125 mL to ¾ cup / 175 mL of fresh berries, dehydrate them for 24 hours, and then pound them in as well. Pemmican is not difficult to make; you just need to start a couple of days before you want to eat it.

1   Make the curing mixture by combining the salt, sugar, lemon zest, and chamomile in a large bowl.

2   Pour half the curing mixture into a large baking pan — big enough to accommodate the salmon fillet and with sides high enough to contain everything. Lay the salmon skin-side down on the base and then cover it with the remaining curing mixture. Cover loosely with plastic wrap and refrigerate for 24 hours.

3   Remove the pan from the refrigerator and rinse the salmon under cool running water for several minutes to wash off all of the curing mixture. Pat the fish dry with a clean cloth or paper towel. >>

1½ cups / 375 mL curing salt

1½ cups / 375 mL packed brown sugar

Zest of 2 lemons

2 tbsp / 30 mL dried chamomile flowers (6 bags of chamomile tea, opened)

1 × 3-lb / 1.4-kg organic Chinook salmon, skin on and pinboned

½ tsp / 2.5 mL freshly ground white pepper

½ cup / 125 mL rendered duck or bacon fat, softened

4   Place the fish, skin-side down, on a cutting board. Using a very sharp, long knife and starting at the tail, cut into the flesh crosswise and carefully shave off thin slices (about ⅛ inch / 3 mm thick). It helps to dip the knife in hot water every few slices.

5   Arrange the salmon slices in a single layer on the dehydrator trays. Set the temperature to 140°F / 60°C and let dry for at least 12 hours or until the salmon is crackly when you bend it but not so dry that it snaps.

6   Place the dried salmon in a food processor and blend until very fine in texture, like breadcrumbs. Transfer the dried salmon to the bowl of a large mortar and pestle and grind it until coarse, like sand. Add the white pepper.

7   Using your hands, work the fat evenly into the salmon just until softened (the heat from your hands should do the trick).

8   Place the mixture onto a sheet of plastic wrap and shape into a log that's about 10 inches / 25 cm long and 1½ inch / 4 cm wide, like a salami. Wrap tightly in the plastic, twisting at both ends. Secure the ends with clips or twist ties, and refrigerate for at least 6 hours or overnight. If you don't plan on using the pemmican right away, freeze it for up to 4 months.

9   To serve, cut the frozen pemmican into thin slices (it's easier to cut when frozen). Return the rest, tightly wrapped, to the fridge or freezer. Let the slices thaw before serving.

**YOU CAN PURCHASE DEHYDRATORS** at local fish and wildlife stores, as well as home and hardware stores. Alternatively, you can lay the fish (and saskatoon berries) on fine-mesh wire racks set on cookie sheets and dry them in the oven. Use your oven's lowest setting and leave the oven door open a crack. Leave the salmon (and berries) inside for 12 hours to dry.

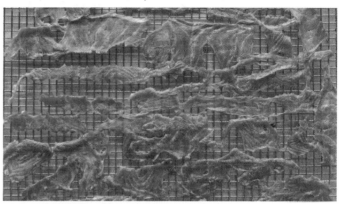

# SALMON THREE WAYS: CURED, "STAINED GLASS," AND SALMON AND EGG SALAD

MAKES 8 TO 10 SERVINGS

This trio of salmon is delicious and impressive. Ensure your salmon is of impeccably high quality and sashimi grade. You'll need to start making this dish at least one or two days in advance, but it's worth the work.

Although this dish is fairly intricate, it's completely doable at home if you can source some Activa GS, an edible transglutaminase "meat glue" sold at specialty food shops and chef shops. You'll also need curing salts.

## Cured Salmon

SPECIAL INGREDIENTS: CURING SALTS

2 cups / 500 mL curing salts (see Tip)

2 cups / 500 mL whole coriander seed

2 cups / 500 mL granulated sugar

2 cups / 500 mL fresh dill, fronds and stems, coarsely chopped

1 × 2 lb / 900-g sashimi-grade Chinook salmon fillet, skin on, pinboned

1    Combine the curing salts, coriander seed, sugar, and dill in a large bowl.

2    Pour half the curing mixture into a baking pan or baking sheet—big enough to accommodate the salmon fillet and with sides high enough to contain everything. Lay the salmon skin-side down on the base and then cover it with the remaining curing mixture. Cover loosely with plastic wrap and refrigerate for 24 hours (or up to 48 hours). Brush the curing salts, coriander, and dill off, reserving the mixture for the stained glass salmon (recipe follows).

---

**TIPS**

Curing salts (a mix of sea salt and sodium nitrite) are available at butcher stores and some specialty kitchen stores, as well as online. They are often dyed reddish pink so as not to be confused with regular sea salt (do not confuse with pink Himalayan salt).

---

Our best bet to acquire Activa GS is to order it online. It is generally sold in 3.5-oz / 100-g packages.

# "Stained Glass" Salmon

SPECIAL INGREDIENTS: ACTIVA GS

1 × 2-lb / 900-g sashimi-grade Chinook or Skuna
  salmon fillet, skin off and pinboned

Reserved curing mixture (from Cured Salmon,
  page 89)

1 cup / 250 mL beet juice (about 2 large red
  beets, peeled and juiced)

Activa GS (see Tip on page 89)

1   Using a sharp knife, cut the salmon fillet
    lengthwise into four 1-inch- / 2.5-cm-wide
    strips.

2   Pour half the curing mixture into a baking
    sheet or pan that accommodates the salmon
    strips and with sides high enough to contain
    everything. Lay the salmon strips on the
    base and then cover with the remaining
    curing mixture. Cover loosely with plastic
    wrap and refrigerate for 24 hours.

3   Remove the pan from the fridge and brush
    off and discard the curing salts. Carefully
    pour the beet juice over the cured salmon
    strips. Cover and refrigerate for at least
    another 15 minutes.

4   Remove the pan from the fridge and drain
    off and discard the beet juice. Pat the salmon
    strips dry with paper towel (it's important
    that the salmon is quite dry). Place the strips
    on a large piece of plastic wrap. Using a pastry
    brush, paint the Activa GS onto all sides of
    the salmon strips. Working quickly, arrange
    two salmon strips side by side so they're just
    touching along the edges, and then stack the
    other two strips on top of them. Stretch the
    plastic wrap over the salmon stacks and wrap
    tightly, like you're making a sushi roll. Twist
    the ends to seal. (Sometimes it helps to release
    any air pockets by poking a tiny hole in the
    plastic wrap with the tip of a sharp knife.)
    Refrigerate for at least an hour.

# Salmon and Egg Salad

1 × 10-oz / 285-g sushi-grade salmon, skin off,
  pinboned, and cut into ½-inch / 1-cm cubes

4 eggs, hard-boiled, peeled, and cut into
  ¼-inch / 0.5-cm dice

¼ cup / 60 mL diced white onion

½ English cucumber, unpeeled, cut into
  ¼-inch / 0.5-cm dice

¾ tsp / 3 mL chopped fresh dill fronds

¼ cup / 60 mL mayonnaise

Salt and freshly ground black pepper, to taste

1   Combine the cubed salmon and diced
    hard-boiled eggs, onion, cucumber, dill,
    mayonnaise, and salt and pepper in a large
    bowl. Stir well. Cover and refrigerate until
    ready to use.

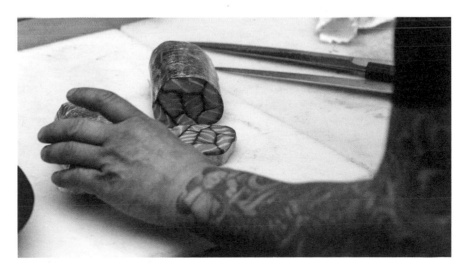

# Plating your trio

SPECIAL EQUIPMENT: 2-INCH / 5-CM RING MOLD (OPTIONAL)

1 tbsp pulverized dried seaweed

Cold-pressed canola oil

1    Using a sharp knife and working across the grain, cut several slices of the cured salmon about ⅛ inch / 3 mm thick. (It helps to dip the knife in hot water every few slices.) Arrange a mound of cured salmon onto one side of each serving plate and sprinkle with the pulverized dried seaweed.

2    Dip a very sharp knife in hot water. Keeping the plastic wrap on the "stained glass" salmon, cut four ¾-inch / 2-cm rounds. Remove the plastic wrap and place one round per plate.

3    If you have a 2-inch / 5-cm ring mold, this is the perfect time to use it: Position the ring mold on your serving plate and press a portion of salmon and egg salad into it. Carefully remove the ring mold and repeat on the remaining serving plates. If you don't have a ring mold, neatly scoop about ⅓ cup / 80 mL of salmon salad onto each serving plate. Drizzle with the oil.

# SEARED SALMON WITH PICKLED CARROTS, CRACKED WILD RICE, AND BEE POLLEN

MAKES 6 TO 8 SERVINGS

Chinook salmon (*Oncorhynchus tshawytscha*), also known as spring salmon, king salmon, and black or blackmouth salmon, are the largest of the Pacific salmon and can grow up to 100 lbs / 45 kg but on average weigh in at about 30 lbs / 13 kg. They're lovely and loaded with fat, which means loads of flavour. That's why you don't need to do much to them, other than cook them. The tang of the pickles is a nice foil for the rich, fatty salmon.

FOR THE RICE

1 cup / 250 mL wild rice

3 cups / 750 mL Pheasant Broth (recipe page 280), fish broth, or chicken broth

Salt, to taste

2 tbsp / 30 mL butter

FOR THE CARROTS

½ cup / 125 mL white wine vinegar

½ cup / 125 mL water

⅓ cup / 80 mL good-quality organic honey (see page 134)

2 tbsp / 30 mL granulated sugar

2 large carrots, peeled

FOR THE SALMON

1 × 2 ½-lb / 1.3-kg Chinook salmon, skin on and pinboned, cut into individual portions

Salt and freshly ground black pepper, to taste

1 tbsp / 15 mL canola oil

¼ cup / 60 mL bee pollen (see sidebar on page 94)

18 to 22 watercress leaves

1   *Prepare the rice:* Preheat the oven to 350° / 175°C (see Tip on page 94).

2   Combine the rice, broth, and a big pinch of salt. Cook over medium-high heat for 45 minutes, until the rice is tender. Season with salt and finish with the butter. Set aside.

3   *Make the pickled carrots:* In a medium pot, combine the vinegar, water, honey, and sugar and bring to a boil. Cook until the liquid has reduced by half, about 15 minutes. >>

4   Using a vegetable peeler, cut the carrot lengthwise into ribbons. Place the ribbons in a heatproof bowl and pour the reduced vinegar mixture over top. Cover and refrigerate.

5   *Prepare the salmon:* Using a sharp knife, cut the salmon into 6-oz / 170-g pieces and season with salt and pepper.

6   Heat the oil in a heavy nonstick skillet over medium-high heat until it shimmers. Place the salmon pieces skin-side down and cook until golden brown, about 4 minutes. Transfer the pan to the preheated oven and continue cooking for 4 to 6 minutes, until the fish is fully translucent and flakes easily with a fork. Remove the pan from the oven and immediately transfer the cooked salmon to a plate to stop the cooking.

7   For each serving, scoop some wild rice onto a plate and top with a piece of salmon. Top with a generous pile of the pickled carrots and sprinkle with bee pollen and a few watercress leaves. Serve immediately.

---

**TIP**

If you are using a conventional oven, you may need to either cook the salmon a little longer or increase the oven temperature by 25°F / 4°C.

**BEE POLLEN** is a protein- and vitamin-packed natural superfood, which is why I like to use it as a garnish in a lot of my recipes, especially salads. It also provides a slight crunchy and nutty texture, plus a lovely hit of bright yellow. Find it at health food stores or online from reputable producers.

Above: Fish being dried the traditional way in Fort Chipewyan, northern Alberta.
Below: Cooking a chum salmon feast at REDx Talks in Vancouver, B.C., in 2016.

# Smoked Chum Salmon Hanging from Driftwood

When I worked with the Haida — a seafaring Nation that has lived in communities on Canada's West Coast islands for at least 13,000 years — I was gifted chum salmon (*Oncorhynchus keta*) for an event in Vancouver in 2016. I decided to cure the salmon in a basic salt-sugar-spice mixture for 24 hours and then cold smoke it for several more hours.

I was feeding a large crowd and wanted to remind people of a more basic way to share food. So to present the smoked chum, I cut off the heads and filleted the salmon, removing the spine but leaving the sides still attached at the tail. My crew and I hung the salmon, tail up, over planks of driftwood. We then instructed everyone just to grab pieces of salmon with their hands and enjoy it.

All of the Elders did, but the youth didn't. It showed me that we need to teach the kids about the traditions again.

Chum is a big Pacific salmon, with light-pink meat and a strong smell. Some people consider it bottom-rung salmon because it's very fatty and not considered much of a delicacy, unlike other varieties of West Coast salmon. The Haida, however, believe in its sustainability, and they told me that they eat chum because it's the largest of the salmon. Its jaw is big and menacing. It has to battle hard through rivers to spawn. It has to fight, fight, fight. And they believe that the energy from the fish will enter your mind and your soul; that when you eat it, you gain its strength and become a stronger person.

Whether you believe that or not, it's still a good story.

# TORCHED PERCH

MAKES 2 TO 4 SERVINGS

When I need to relax, I go fishing. I love cooking whole fish. I created this recipe as a way to have a bit of fun with presentation. You can make this recipe using freshwater yellow perch (*Perca flavescens*) or ocean perch (*Sebastes marinus*), as seen in the photo (previous page).

1   Heat a grill to 450°F / 230°C.

2   In a dry pan over medium heat, toast the pickling spice until fragrant and the spices turn brown. Remove the pan from the heat and transfer the toasted spices to a plate immediately to stop the cooking. Let cool.

3   Transfer the cooled pickling spice to a food processor and pulse to a rough dust. Pour into a bowl and stir in the oil, parsley, garlic, salt, and pepper. Set aside.

4   Using a sharp knife, score the fish skin on both sides, making 4 or 5 cuts from the dorsal (top) of the fish toward its stomach. Stuff the rosemary into the mouth and trim so that only 2 to 3 inches / 5 to 8 cm protrudes.

5   Rub the spice paste onto the fish, but be very careful of the fish's sharp fins.

6   Brush the hot grill with oil. Place the prepared fish on the hot grill. Grill for about 5 minutes on each side, brushing with more oil as it cooks, until the flesh is opaque (check the inside of the score marks on each side to ensure fish is cooked through).

7   Meanwhile, place the lemon halves cut-side down on the grill and cook until they take on good char marks and the lemons soften.

8   Serve the fish whole, with the seared lemon halves alongside. Let people break off sections of the fish with a fork and remind them to spritz each mouthful of fish with a squeeze of lemon before eating.

¾ cup / 175 mL pickling spice (see page 166)

¾ cup / 175 mL neutral-flavoured cooking oil (such as canola), to oil the grill and the fish

½ bunch fresh parsley, finely chopped

1 tbsp / 15 mL minced garlic

1 tsp / 5 mL salt

½ tsp / 2.5 mL freshly ground black pepper

1 whole perch, cleaned and descaled

8 sprigs fresh rosemary

2 lemons, cut in half widthwise

# TROUT CAKES IN DILL SAUCE WITH CRISPY POTATO CHIPS

MAKES 4 SERVINGS | SPECIAL EQUIPMENT: 3-INCH / 7.5-CM RING MOLDS (OPTIONAL); DEEP-FRY THERMOMETER

This satisfying summer meal — with a meaty trout cake, fresh dill sauce, and crunchy homemade potato chips — is simple to make but stunning on the plate. In a professional kitchen, we use stainless steel ring molds about 3 inches / 7.5 cm in diameter by 1½ inches / 3.5 cm high — to form the cakes. If you don't have these, you can use a small, round, cleaned-out can (like the kind tuna and salmon are sold in) that has been opened on both ends, or simply use your hands to form more rustic fish cakes. Whichever method you use, they'll look amazing and taste delicious.

The homemade potato chips are certain to become a favourite crunchy garnish. The dressing is actually a version of Cobb salad dressing. (You'll end up with more than you need, but keep the rest for a fresh green salad … either at the same meal or the next.) The dill sauce is equally amazing with any sort of smoked fish, like gravlax or smoked sablefish.

### FOR THE POTATO CHIPS

1 Yukon Gold potato, unpeeled

¼ cup / 60 mL white vinegar

3 cups / 750 mL canola oil, for frying

1 tbsp / 15 mL fleur de sel

### FOR THE DRESSING

1 tsp / 5 mL ground cinnamon

1 tbsp / 15 mL ground cayenne

½ tsp / 2.5 mL ground cumin

1 cup / 250 mL mayonnaise

½ cup / 125 mL whipping (35%) cream

¼ cup / 60 mL good-quality organic honey (see page 134)

¼ cup / 60 mL water

### FOR THE DILL SAUCE

½ cup / 125 mL fresh dill

½ cup / 125 mL mayonnaise

½ cup / 125 mL extra virgin olive oil

½ cup / 125 mL water

2 tbsp / 30 mL raw sesame seeds

### FOR THE TROUT CAKES

4 small trout fillets (about 1 lb / 450 g total)

1 cup / 250 mL plain panko crumbs

2 tbsp / 30 mL neutral-flavoured cooking oil (such as canola), for frying

2 tbsp / 30 mL cold-pressed canola oil, for drizzling

3 tbsp / 45 mL chopped fresh herbs of your choice, for garnish

1 lemon, quartered lengthwise, for serving

1   *Prepare the potatoes:* Set your mandoline slicer to its thinnest setting, ideally ⅛ inch / 3 mm, or use a sharp knife to thinly slice the potato. As you cut them, transfer the potato slices to a large bowlful of cold water. Give the potatoes a gentle stir and then drain. Refresh the water and then drain again, repeating the process until all the starch has washed off the potato slices and the water runs clear. Fill the bowl with water one more time and add the vinegar. Set aside while you make the dressing and sauce.

2   *Make the dressing:* Gently toast the cinnamon, cayenne, and cumin in a dry pan over medium heat for a couple of minutes, just until fragrant. Transfer the toasted spices to a medium bowl and stir in the mayonnaise, whipping cream, honey, and water; mix well. Cover and refrigerate until needed.

3   *Make the dill sauce:* Combine the dill, mayonnaise, olive oil, water, and sesame seeds in a blender and purée until smooth. Cover and refrigerate until needed.

4   *Cook the potatoes:* Drain the potato slices and arrange them in a single layer on paper towel; pat the tops dry. Fill a heavy pot with 3 to 4 inches / 8 to 10 cm of oil and heat to 300°F / 150°C. Working in two or three batches (you don't want to crowd them), fry each batch for about 5 minutes, until golden. Using a wire-mesh scoop or slotted spoon, transfer the fried chips to paper towel, shaking off as much oil as you safely can. Sprinkle evenly with fleur de sel. Let cool completely and store at room temperature.

5   *Make the trout cakes:* Preheat the oven to 350°F / 180°C (see Tip).

6   Place the trout fillets skin-side down on a cutting board. Using a very sharp knife and cutting across the grain, shave off thin slices, stopping right at the skin. Flake the fish apart with your hands into a mixing bowl. Add about 2 tbsp / 30 mL of the dressing, or just enough so the fish holds together when gently squeezed.

7   Divide the mixture into 4 equal portions. Spread the panko on a shallow plate. If you happen to have ring molds, lightly oil the insides and scoop each portion into the molds, packing gently, then press the exposed top and bottom of the fish cake into the panko crumbs to evenly cover both ends. If you don't have ring molds (and aren't using the tuna-can hack), use your hands to shape each portion into a patty and coat the top and bottom in panko.

> **TIP**
>
> If you are using a conventional oven, you may need to either cook the dish a little longer or increase the oven temperature by 25°F / 4°C.

8    In a cast iron or ovenproof skillet, heat a drizzle of oil over medium-high heat. Carefully place the breaded cakes into the pan and cook until golden on the bottom, 3 to 4 minutes. Using a flipping spatula or fish slice, gently turn the cakes over. Immediately put the skillet into the preheated oven and cook for about 5 minutes. Check one of the cakes for doneness by probing into the centre with a small knife. The fish should be opaque. As soon as the fish cakes are cooked through, transfer them to a plate to ensure they don't overcook.

9    Place ¼ cup / 60 mL of the dill sauce in the bottom of four serving bowls. Arrange a trout cake in each bowl. Drizzle with cold-pressed canola oil and garnish with the crispy potato chips and fresh herbs. Serve with a lemon wedge.

# WEST COAST ALBACORE TUNA WITH CREAMED CORN, RED ONION PETALS, HORSERADISH CHIPS, AND GREENS

MAKES 2 TO 4 SERVINGS (AS AN APPETIZER) | SPECIAL EQUIPMENT: DEEP-FRY THERMOMETER

I'm very inspired by flowers, and I knew right away that I wanted this dish to have the freshness of a newly opened water lily. Inside the "petals," delicate tuna and sweet cream are a nice contrast to the crunch of pungent horseradish chips, the saltiness of the seaweed, and the delicate pop of microgreens.

1  Combine the corn and broth in a small pot. Bring to a gentle boil over medium heat and cook until the liquid has reduced by half, about 5 minutes. Stir in the cream and cook until reduced by half again, another 5 minutes. Add the garlic and shallot, and remove the pan from the heat. Let cool. Transfer to a blender and purée until smooth. Set aside.

2  Make an ice water bath (a large bowl filled with cold water and ice cubes). Bring a small pot of water to a boil. Add the horseradish strips to the boiling water and cook for about 1 minute. Using a wire-mesh scoop or slotted spoon, transfer the strips to the ice bath for a few seconds. Remove and squeeze out any excess water. Pat dry with paper towel.

3  Fill a heavy pot with about 2 inches / 5 cm of oil and preheat to 350°F / 180°C. Fry the horseradish strips until golden brown, 3 or 4 minutes. Using a wire-mesh scoop or slotted spoon, transfer the fried strips to paper towel and season with a pinch of fleur de sel. Set aside. >>

½ cup / 125 mL corn kernels (fresh or frozen)

¼ cup / 60 mL Pheasant Broth (recipe page 280) or good-quality chicken broth

¼ cup / 60 mL whipping (35%) cream

1 tbsp / 15 mL minced garlic

1 tbsp / 15 mL minced shallot

1 fresh horseradish root, peeled and cut into long ribbons (see Tip on page 106)

3 cups / 750 mL + 2 tbsp / 30 mL canola oil, divided (approx.)

Fleur de sel

1 medium red onion

2-inch / 5-cm length of Albacore tuna loin

1 tbsp / 15 mL cold-pressed hemp oil

2 to 3 tbsp / 30 to 45 mL radish microgreens

2 tsp / 10 mL crushed or crumbled wakame or other dried seaweed flakes (see sidebar on page 106)

4   Cut the red onion in half lengthwise, from tip to bottom. Carefully separate the layers of each half (each portion should look like a little bowl or petal; you'll end up with 4 to 6 petals). Pour 2 tbsp (30 mL) of vegetable oil into a heavy skillet over medium-high heat. Fry the onion petals on both sides just enough to brown them but not so much that they lose their shape (they should be translucent and flexible but still cup-shaped).

5   Cut the tuna loin into ½- to ¾-inch / 1- to 2-cm cubes (it's easier to cut while frozen). You'll want about ¼ cup / 60 mL of diced tuna, tightly packed. If you don't use the whole piece, rewrap and freeze the rest of the loin for another occasion.

6   Arrange the onion bowls in a water lily configuration on a round serving platter. Pour about 1 tbsp / 15 mL of the creamed corn purée into the cup of each red onion. Place a heaping tablespoon of diced tuna onto the purée in each cup.

7   To garnish, drizzle the hemp oil over the onion petals and sprinkle with a few radish microgreens and a crumble of the fried horseradish. Top with the crushed wakame or other dried seaweed. Serve at room temperature.

**WAKAME** is an edible seaweed that is sold dried in many Asian specialty grocers and well-stocked grocery stores. It is also widely available online and directly from harvesters on the Pacific and Atlantic coasts in Canada and the United States. Wakame has a slightly firm, gelatinous texture, and can have a sweet note. (You will recognize it as the greenish-brown pieces of seaweed in miso soup.) If you can't find wakame, experiment with other varieties of crushed or crumbled dried seaweed.

---
**TIP**

Use a Y-peeler to cut long strips of horseradish.

---

# DUNGENESS CRAB WITH GRILLED OYSTER MUSHROOMS

MAKES 2 SERVINGS

I had an incredible experience visiting Gingolx, a remote community in northern British Columbia, and this dish is based on my experiences there. The mountains run right into the ocean so ingredients are very limited — and the closest grocery store is a four-and-a-half-hour drive. Out of necessity and sheer abundance, the Nisga'a source much of their food from the sea and surrounding area. Pairing crab with mushrooms is a natural and delicious fit.

Lucky for the rest of us, most commercially available crabmeat is sustainably harvested and fairly easy to obtain.

1   Preheat the grill to medium (350°F / 180°C).

2   Brush the mushroom bunches with the melted butter and season with the salt and pepper. Grill, turning occasionally, just until soft, about 5 minutes. Set aside to cool.

3   In a bowl, combine the crabmeat, onion, and parsley, and stir until the crabmeat becomes a bit stringy and is well integrated. Break apart the cooled mushroom bunches and stir them into the crab and onion mixture.

4   Arrange on a serving plate in any way you wish (I like making a Z-shaped pattern). Garnish with watercress leaves. Serve immediately.

14 oz / 400 g (about 4) oyster mushroom bunches

2 tbsp / 30 mL butter, melted

¼ tsp / 1 mL each salt and freshly ground black pepper

1 lb / 450 g Dungeness crabmeat

¼ cup / 60 mL finely diced white onion

¼ cup / 60 mL finely minced fresh parsley leaves

½ cup / 125 mL watercress

This page and overleaf:
Dancers at the National Indigenous Peoples Day
Celebration on June 21, 2018, in Edmonton, Alberta.

# POW WOW

The Enoch Cree Nation annual Pow Wow Celebration takes place over two days in mid-July. All are welcome.

**MANY PEOPLE DON'T REALIZE** that pow wow is not just for First Nations peoples. Anyone can go. It's a festival. There are competitions. There are games. There are dancers. It's exciting and energizing. It's an alcohol-free celebration. Everyone is welcome.

That said, it's really hard for me to convince my friends to attend pow wow or round dances. I guess people who have never attended one are worried that they won't be welcomed, or that they'll make a mistake or feel uncomfortable. I'd encourage anyone who wants to attend to go: Be respectful, ask questions politely if you want, and then just enjoy yourself.

Pow wows will be slightly different in each community, but there's an order to the events and competitions, areas for spectators, and areas for Elders and competitors. There are also some parts of the program where it will be disrespectful to film or photograph. You can find out what the etiquette expectations are by connecting with the local band and asking questions.

# SKEWERED BISON STRIPS

MAKES 4 SERVINGS | SPECIAL EQUIPMENT: 10 TO 12 BAMBOO SKEWERS, SOAKED IN WATER OVERNIGHT

I really love Japanese food and street food. It inspires me when I'm dreaming about Indigenous cooking. Imagine going to pow wow and being able to get bison skewers. People would go crazy for them. Maybe one day this dream will be a reality.

If you wish, you can prepare the meat and let it marinate overnight; however, it will take on a very deep garlic flavour. If you prefer a lighter garlic taste, prepare the meat an hour or so before you want to start cooking.

1   In a bowl, combine the bison, oil, garlic, and salt and pepper. Toss to coat the strips of meat evenly. Cover and refrigerate overnight, or let sit at room temperature if you will be cooking the skewers in an hour or so.

2   Preheat the grill to high (400°F / 200°C). Brush the grill with oil.

3   Carefully thread the meat onto the soaked skewers, starting at one end and piercing through the meat every 2 inches / 5 cm or so. Place the skewers on the grill and cook just until there is some browning on the meat and it's just beyond the pink stage, about 5 minutes. (Be careful not to overcook.) Serve immediately, with rosemary sprigs for garnish (if using).

1 × 1-lb / 450-g bison sirloin, cut against the grain into ⅛-inch / 3-mm slices

¼ cup / 60 mL canola oil

2 cloves garlic, crushed

½ tsp / 2.5 mL each salt and freshly ground black pepper

Rosemary sprigs, for garnish (optional)

# ONE-POT SPAGHETTI SQUASH, BISON, AND CORN

MAKES 4 SERVINGS | SPECIAL EQUIPMENT: SLOW COOKER

Cooked spaghetti squash is nice and soft. I like how when you dig into this dish with your spoon, you can get a little taste of everything — the squash, the bison, and the corn.

1   Combine the brisket, onion, garlic and shallot mix, and bison broth in the bowl of a slow cooker. Cover and cook on Low for 12 hours or on High for 6 hours.

2   Transfer the cooked brisket to a platter and set aside to cool; discard cooking liquid.

3   About an hour before serving, preheat the oven to 400°F / 200°C (see Tip on page 112).

4   Using a cleaver or a large, sharp knife, cut the spaghetti squash in half from the stem to the bottom end. Leave the seeds inside. Sprinkle the flesh side with the cinnamon, nutmeg, and salt. Place cut-side down on a baking sheet. Cook for 30 to 40 minutes, until the squash is fork-tender but still firm throughout. Remove the pan from the oven and set aside until the squash is cool enough to handle. Using a large spoon, gently scoop out and discard the seeds, leaving the flesh of the squash intact in the shells. Set aside.

1 × 1½-lb / 680-g bison brisket

1 large white onion, roughly chopped into wedges

1 tbsp / 15 mL Minced Garlic and Shallots in Oil (recipe page 282)

2 cups / 500 mL Bison Bone Broth (recipe page 276)

1 large spaghetti squash (3 lbs / 1.4 kg)

¼ tsp / 1 mL ground cinnamon

¼ tsp / 1 mL ground nutmeg

1 tsp / 5 mL salt

1 tsp / 5 mL neutral-flavoured cooking oil (such as canola)

1½ cups / 375 mL corn kernels (fresh or frozen)

Salt and freshly ground black pepper, to taste

¼ cup / 60 mL dried rose petals (optional)

5   Shred the brisket using two forks with their backs
    facing one another (pull the forks in opposite
    directions to shred the meat). Place the shredded
    brisket in a large skillet (10 inches / 25 cm in
    diameter or larger to hold all the meat) over medium
    heat with the oil. Stir in the corn and cook for
    another few minutes, just to warm everything
    through. Season with salt and pepper.

6   To serve, spoon equal amounts of the shredded bison
    and corn inside each of the two halves of squash.
    Garnish with the rose petals (if using). Serve hot,
    family-style.

───── TIP ─────

If you are using a
conventional oven, you may
need to either cook the dish
a little longer or increase
the oven temperature by
25°F / 4°C.

# SALT-ROASTED BEET AND GOAT CHEESE SALAD WITH CANDIED PISTACHIOS

MAKES 4 SERVINGS | SPECIAL EQUIPMENT: RUBBER OR LATEX GLOVES (OPTIONAL)

We often ate this salad during our marathon days in the kitchen creating and recipe testing for this book. It's tangy, earthy, and sweet all at once. That's why it's so good. It takes a number of steps to prepare, but you can do some of them the day before. And if there is some leftover dressing, it's great on green salad as well, or drizzled on any of your favourite roasted vegetables.

### FOR THE ROASTED BEETS

6 cups / 1.5 L coarse kosher salt

6 medium red and yellow beets, leaves and roots trimmed

### FOR THE DRESSING

½ cup / 125 mL balsamic vinegar

1½ cups / 375 mL mayonnaise

1 tsp / 5 mL minced garlic

1 tbsp / 15 mL Worcestershire sauce

½ cup / 125 mL pure maple syrup

### FOR THE CANDIED PISTACHIOS

2 cups / 500 mL neutral-flavoured cooking oil (such as canola), for frying

1 cup / 250 mL unsalted pistachios

¾ cup / 175 mL icing sugar

### FOR SERVING

4 oz / 115 g soft goat cheese (about ½ cup / 125 mL)

1   *Roast the beets:* Preheat the oven to 400°F / 200°C (see Tip on page 122).

2   Pour a ¾-inch / 2-cm layer of the salt into a baking dish just large enough to hold all of the beets. Place the beets root-end up on the salt bed. Cover with the remaining salt and bake for about an hour.

3   Remove the pan from the oven and let cool for about 15 minutes. The salt turns into a hard crust, and the beets hold in the moisture, so be careful as there might still be steam trapped. Carefully remove the beets from the salt and brush off any excess. Peel the skin with your fingers (it should slip off; you may want to wear rubber or latex gloves to avoid staining your hands). Rinse quickly under cool running water. Slice the peeled beets on the thin setting of a mandoline, about ⅛ inch / 3 mm. Transfer to a resealable container, cover, and refrigerate until ready to use. >>

4   *Make the dressing:* Whisk together the balsamic vinegar, mayonnaise, garlic, Worcestershire, and maple syrup in a small bowl.

5   *Candy the pistachios:* Fill a saucepan with 1½ inches / 3.5 cm of oil and heat to 300°F / 150°C.

6   Meanwhile, in another saucepan of boiling water, blanch the pistachios for 30 seconds. Using a fine-mesh sieve, drain the pistachios (give them a few flicks of the wrist to dry them out as they cool) and transfer to a small bowl. Add the icing sugar and toss to coat well. Fry the sugared pistachios in the hot oil for 1 minute or until golden. Using a wire-mesh scoop, transfer them to paper towel to drain and cool.

7   To serve, divide the beets among 4 serving plates and arrange in an overlapping pattern. Drizzle with the dressing and garnish with crumbled goat cheese and the candied pistachios.

---
**TIP**

If you are using a conventional oven, you may need to either cook the items a little longer or increase the oven temperature by 25°F / 4°C.

---

# SWEET POTATO SALAD

MAKES 2 TO 4 SERVINGS

Sweet potatoes are delicious in salad. I like to roast mine in the skin, but you can peel yours, if you like. North American grocery stores typically carry a few varieties of sweet potatoes — some are small and oblong with yellow or dark-orange flesh, and some are larger. Darker sweet potatoes with orange flesh are often mislabelled as yams. True yams, however, are very starchy, pale-fleshed tubers with a dark-brown, bark-like skin and are usually not readily available outside of specialty grocery stores. You want sweet potatoes for this recipe.

### FOR THE VINAIGRETTE

¼ cup / 60 mL extra virgin olive oil

2 tbsp / 30 mL sherry vinegar or white wine vinegar

2 tbsp / 30 mL red wine vinegar

½ tsp / 2.5 mL salt

¼ tsp / 1 mL freshly ground black pepper

1 sprig fresh parsley (curly or flat-leaf), finely chopped

1 tbsp / 15 mL minced garlic

### FOR THE SALAD

2 to 3 medium sweet potatoes (about 20 oz / 600 g total)

2 tbsp / 30 mL cold-pressed canola oil

1 large kale leaf

½ English cucumber

5 sprigs fresh parsley (curly or flat-leaf), leaves only

6 watercress leaves

### FOR SERVING

3 tbsp / 45 mL mossberries or saskatoon berries, for garnish

Fleur de sel, to taste

1   Preheat the oven to 400°F / 200°C (see Tip on page 124). Line a baking sheet with parchment paper.

2   *Make the vinaigrette:* Combine the olive oil, sherry vinegar, red wine vinegar, salt, pepper, finely chopped parsley, and minced garlic in a small jar and shake well. Set aside.

3   *Make the salad:* Cut the sweet potatoes in half (or quarters, if large) and place cut-side down on the prepared baking sheet. Using a knife, pierce the skin a few times on each half. >>

4   Bake in the preheated oven for 25 to 45 minutes
    (depending on size of sweet potatoes), until the
    skin easily separates from the soft flesh. Remove the
    roasted sweet potatoes from the oven and set aside
    until cool enough to handle.

5   Using your fingers, peel the skin off the sweet
    potatoes (and discard skin). Cut the flesh into
    1-inch / 2.5-cm cubes. Toss with oil. Set aside.

6   Remove the tough ribs from the kale leaf and
    cut into bite-size pieces. Slice the cucumber into
    ¼-inch / 0.5-cm coins.

7   Scatter the prepared sweet potato, kale, cucumbers,
    parsley, and watercress on a serving platter. Shake the
    vinaigrette well and drizzle over the salad. Garnish
    with the mossberries and some fleur de sel. Serve
    immediately.

---

**TIP**

If you are using a
conventional oven, you
may need to either cook
the sweet potatoes a little
longer or increase the oven
temperature by 25°F / 4°C.

---

# POTATOES BOILED IN GARLIC CREAM

MAKES 4 TO 6 SERVINGS (AS A SIDE DISH)

There's so much boiled food in Indigenous cuisine — it's one of the main food preparation techniques. This dish is a fancy version of so much of the simple, boiled food that our communities eat, yet it's an example of how truly good simple can be. The silky potatoes bathed in sweet and garlic-tinted cream could be a meal on their own. Or serve them with a crispy, pan-fried fish fillet or with a bison pot roast or a simple roast chicken.

If you decide to reserve the warm cream leftover from cooking the potatoes, it's great over seafood or pasta.

1   In a large pot, combine the potatoes, onion, garlic, whipping cream, half-and-half, and broth. Bring to a simmer over medium heat — watch it carefully: it will make a mess if it boils over — and cook until the potatoes are tender, about 30 minutes (when a toothpick or sharp knife slide in and out of the flesh cleanly, you know they are ready).

2   Strain the cooked potatoes, reserving the warm garlic cream for another use, and transfer to a bowl. Season with salt and the chopped parsley. Serve steaming hot.

4 large Yukon Gold potatoes, peeled or unpeeled, quartered

½ medium white onion, thinly sliced

6 cloves garlic, thinly sliced

2 cups / 500 mL whipping (35%) cream

1 cup / 250 mL half-and-half (10%) cream

1 cup / 250 mL Pheasant Broth (recipe page 280) or good-quality chicken broth

Salt, to taste

¼ cup / 60 mL finely chopped fresh parsley

**WHEN I VISITED GINGOLX,** a seaside Nisga'a community in northern British Columbia, we went hunting for seal. The ocean was way too rough to catch anything that day, but another hunter had gotten a seal the day before. When the community members told me that we were going to boil the seal meat, I thought, *Why would you boil it? It'll just make it tough, rubbery, and tasteless.*

Sure enough, we boiled the seal meat and bones for an hour and a half. Just in water and with some basic diced carrots, onion, and celery, and salt and pepper.

I was put in charge of stirring the meat. I was told you have to stir it constantly for the full time. No stopping.

I only lasted about 20 minutes before others stepped in to take turns, but we did stir it for the entire cooking time. Afterward, we strained the broth and then dipped the boiled seal in it. You know what? It was magical. I've had seal tartare. I've had grilled seal. Boiled seal meat is the best. And it's prepared in exactly the opposite way of how we're taught to prepare meat in culinary school.

# WHEN FOOD IS AND ISN'T MEDICINE

**BECAUSE I WAS ADOPTED** and never met my birth parents, I don't really know my genetic family medical history. When I was diagnosed with type 2 diabetes before my fortieth birthday, however, I can't say I was surprised. It's so prevalent in my community. Studies show that an Indigenous person in Canada has an 80 percent chance of developing type 2 diabetes. That's pretty staggering, especially when you compare this with the general Canadian population, which has a 50 percent chance of getting type 2 diabetes. What's more, Indigenous people develop it at an earlier age than the rest of the population.

A lot of Indigenous people don't really know much about Indigenous food. I'm not poking fun at my own people. It's a fact. You go to pow wow and what do you see? Indian tacos, bannock, burgers, fries, poutine, pop, potato chips — everything that is bad for you. You can't even get a glass of milk. (I wouldn't mind a glass of milk at a pow wow from time to time.) I get it: It's a carnival and it's fun, but including some Indigenous smokehouse food, such as smoked salmon, fish, brisket, and bison wouldn't be hard. I'm hopeful we'll soon see these kinds of foods offered at our celebrations.

Part of what I'm having to do is learn to take care of my body again — and our Nations need to do the same. We have a long way to go. I'm relatively young and not overweight enough to be type 2 diabetic, but I see how unhealthy diets and weight gain affects our people. I see people in our communities with big middles and skinny legs — we're clearly not able to handle all the fat and refined carbohydrates in processed foods. We need to change our diets.

I get asked to speak on a variety of topics. Recently, I was asked to speak at a climate change conference. I thought, *What does a*

A rack built for smoking, cooking, and drying meat and fish on the property of Violet Cardinal, in Lac La Biche, Alberta.

*chef know about climate change?* It took me a while to figure out what I was going to say. After some thought, I made this connection: Humans are causing climate change through our bad decisions. So what do we need to make better decisions? Well, among many things, we need a healthy diet. Our food choices affect our thoughts, our personalities, our ups and our downs. What we put into our bodies affects how we make decisions and even what those decisions are.

The main keynote speaker at the conference was Dr. Willie Littlechild, a prominent lawyer and former athlete, and a residential school survivor. Dr. Littlechild was impressed by my talk, which was very flattering. Afterward he said to me, "I don't know if I should be eating bannock now." (I have included recipes for bannock, also known as fry bread, in this book, but I do caution that the deep-fried version

should only be enjoyed as a treat on special occasions.)

When we eat healthily, we feel better and we make better decisions. If someone is in a position to make policy decisions that affect our environment and our climate, then they should realize a healthy body gives our minds a fighting chance to make good choices. If you're sick, you can't be at your best. You can't have the life you deserve.

*"Part of what I'm having to do is learn to take care of my body again — and our Nations need to do the same."*

# SOAPBERRY WHIP ON FRESH BERRIES

MAKES 8 TO 10 SERVINGS

Soapberries (*Shepherdia canadensis*) are an acquired taste. They contain compounds called saponins that give them a bittersweet flavour which to me is a cross between tomato paste and bitter cherries. When mixed and whipped with water they produce a soapy foam (hence their name). This foam is a traditional food known as "Indian ice cream," and you can sometimes find it served at pow wows. Traditionally, the soapberries are whipped by hand using the fingers as a whisk, which takes patience and arm strength. The berries are too intense for me to eat fresh, but whipped like this into a foam, I find them a perfect topping for sweet wild strawberries, raspberries, or saskatoons.

When I was visiting Gingolx, B.C., and getting my hand-poke tattoo from Nakkita Trimble-Wilson (see page 214), she hand-whipped canned soapberry juice into a foam for me. The technique I describe below is hers, as is the recipe, handed down to Nakkita from her grandmother Jean (Trimble) Fitzgerald, whom she calls Mom, and her great aunt Colleen Barton, whom she calls Gigi. It is important to acknowledge where these recipes come from, for both Nakkita and me.

1 Combine the soapberries and soapberry juice in a medium bowl. Using your hands, squish the berries until all of the additional juices have been released. Using a fine-mesh sieve, strain the liquid into a large (8-cup / 2-L capacity) non-reactive metal or glass bowl. Discard the pulp. Add the water. With your hand hanging loosely in the bowl and your fingers spread apart slightly to form a whisk, whip the berry juice — quickly and continuously — until it forms stiff peaks, about 15 minutes (the foam should be dense).

2 Add the honey and whip for another minute or two. Taste and adjust sweetness, if you like, whipping after each addition of honey. Set aside.

3 Divide the fresh seasonal berries evenly into small serving bowls or glass cups. Top with a tablespoon of soapberry foam. Serve and eat immediately.

1 tbsp / 15 mL fresh soapberries

1 tbsp / 15 mL soapberry juice from canned soapberries (or another 1 tbsp fresh soapberries; if you don't have fresh, you can use 2 tbsp / 30 mL canned soapberries and juice)

5 tbsp / 75 mL water

1 tbsp / 30 mL good quality organic honey, or to taste

4 cups / 1 L fresh seasonal berries, such as saskatoons, raspberries, strawberries or blueberries

### TIP

Both the bowl and your hands must be squeaky clean or the berries won't foam up properly.

**SOAPBERRIES** (also known as russet buffaloberry, Canadian buffaloberry, and soopolallie) grow throughout Canada (except on Prince Edward Island), including the North, as well as across the northern U.S. states, the West Coast, and even Alaska. The shiny red berries ripen on low-lying evergreen shrubs in summer from June to August (depending on where you find them). You can use them fresh, freeze them whole for another day, or make canned soapberries and preserve them in jars for use in making soapberry whip (recipe opposite) or even a soapberry lemonade.

Consume soapberries in moderation: a few fresh berries at a time or just a dollop or so of whipped soapberry foam. The bitter compounds can cause stomach upset if eaten in excess.

# ICED LABRADOR TEA

MAKES 4 SERVINGS

Labrador tea can be brewed from three closely related plants in the heath family: Bog Labrador tea, Northern Labrador tea, and Western Labrador tea grow in bogs and wetland areas in most regions of Canada. People have been brewing soothing teas from their fresh and dried leaves for generations. Western Labrador tea has a more subtle taste than its Eastern counterpart, Bog Labrador tea, which tends to have a stronger, more camphorous aroma. If you can't harvest your own, you can purchase Labrador tea at herbal tea stores or online. It is high in vitamin C and is believed to have important medicinal properties for treating colds, indigestion, sore throats, and fever, but needs to be consumed in moderation (toxicity can occur when it's steeped for too long or if more than several cups per day are ingested).

1   *Make the tea:* Bring 4 cups / 1 L of water to a boil in a saucepan. Reduce the heat to a simmer and add the tea leaves (they'll float on the surface of the water so push them down with a spoon to submerge them a few times during the steeping process). Let steep for about 5 minutes (the tea will be a light-orange colour).

2   *Make the syrup:* Combine the water, honey, lemon juice, mint, rosemary, and cinnamon in a saucepan. Bring to a simmer over medium heat and cook for 10 to 15 minutes. Remove from the heat and, using a fine-mesh sieve, strain well (discard solids). Set aside to cool.

3   To serve, fill a tall glass with ice. Add about ¼ cup / 60 mL of syrup and 1½ cups / 375 mL of brewed tea. Taste and add more syrup if you prefer it a little sweeter.

FOR THE TEA

4 cups / 1 L water

50 to 75 Labrador tea leaves

Ice, for serving

FOR THE SYRUP

¾ cup / 175 mL water

¾ cup / 175 mL good-quality organic honey (see sidebar)

¼ cup / 60 mL freshly squeezed lemon juice

2 tbsp / 30 mL chopped fresh mint

2 sprigs fresh rosemary

1 x 3-inch / 7.5-cm cinnamon stick

## HONEY

Alberta is the top producer of honey in Canada. I'm lucky to have access to beautiful organic wildflower honey directly from beekeepers. Since the flavour of honey changes from place to place, look for the most natural, cleanest source of honey you can find. It's more expensive than bulk honey sold in the supermarket, but you'll be getting a much better-tasting, and likely more healthy, product. If you can, buy your honey directly from the honey producer or as close to where you live as possible. Healthy bees are great for the environment, and buying good, organic honey is a great way to support sustainable and productive apiaries.

ᒋᑲ·ᑭᐤ

takwâkin

# FALL

# FALL

# WARM PUMPKIN SALAD WITH TOASTED PUMPKIN SEEDS AND SEARED CUCUMBER

MAKES 6 TO 8 SERVINGS

Pumpkins and other squash are important crops in Indigenous cooking. The flesh is filling and full of carbohydrates. The seeds are chock full of protein and rich in micronutrients and minerals.

This recipe was created on the fly in the kitchen one day when a pumpkin from Jennifer's mom, Barb Cockrall, arrived as a gift. Warm pumpkin salad is now a go-to fall vegetable dish.

1   Preheat the oven to 350°F / 180°C (see Tip on page 142).

2   Place the pumpkin (whole) on a baking sheet and cook in the preheated oven until soft and slightly caramelized, 45 minutes to 1 hour (the pumpkin should start to sag on top and the flesh under the rind will feel soft to the touch). Remove the pan from the heat and set aside until the pumpkin is cool enough to handle. Using your hands, peel the rind away from the flesh. Discard the strings from the centre but reserve the seeds. Cut the flesh into ¾-inch / 2-cm cubes (you should end up with about 4 cups / 1 L).

3   Rinse the seeds in a colander under cool running water, using your fingers to separate them from the strings. Discard the strings and any lingering pumpkin flesh, and spread the seeds out on paper towel to dry completely.

4   In a small, dry skillet over medium heat, toast the pumpkin seeds until they turn golden, 3 to 5 minutes (they'll pop slightly when fully toasted). Transfer the toasted seeds to a plate immediately. In the same dry skillet, cook the cucumber slices until golden brown around the edges and in the middle, about 5 minutes per side. Set aside. >>

1 medium pumpkin
(about 8 lbs / 3.5 kg)

1 English cucumber, cut into
¼-inch / 0.5-cm rounds

2½ tbsp / 37 mL cold-pressed canola oil, extra virgin olive oil, or pumpkin seed oil

1 tsp / 5 mL finely minced garlic

1 tsp / 5 mL finely minced shallot

6 tbsp / 90 mL good-quality organic honey (see page 134)

Juice of 1 lemon

½ tsp / 2.5 mL salt

½ tsp / 2.5 mL freshly ground black pepper

½ bunch fresh curly parsley, roughly chopped

5   In a large bowl, whisk together the oil, garlic, shallot, honey, lemon juice, salt, and pepper. Add the warm pumpkin cubes and toss until well coated.

6   Serve on a large plate or family-style platter. Sprinkle with about ½ cup / 125 mL of the toasted pumpkin seeds and the chopped parsley, and top with the warm cucumber slices.

> **TIP**
>
> If you are using a conventional oven, you may need to either cook the pumpkin a little longer or increase the oven temperature by 25°F / 4°C.

## TREE SYRUP

Sweet, amber-coloured maple syrup is most often poured over pancakes, but for me it has so many other purposes. I love its caramel flavour but also the roasted and faint vanilla notes, among other things. It's sweet but not as sweet as honey. I always feel like I can taste the trees, and therefore the forest, in high-quality maple syrup.

Birch syrup is less well known but has an interesting, mineral-rich woodsy flavour. It takes 26 U.S. gallons / 100 L of birch sap to make 4 cups / 1 L of syrup, so it's more expensive than maple syrup (maple syrup requires 16 U.S. gallons / 60 L of sap per 4 cups / 1 L of syrup.)

# POACHED SWEET AND SAVOURY AUTUMN APPLES

MAKES 6 SERVINGS | SPECIAL INGREDIENTS: BIRCH SYRUP; PORCINI POWDER

Inspired by the forest in the fall, this is an unlikely yet delicious combination of apples, syrups, vinegar, and powdered mushrooms. Some apples, such as Ambrosia, Granny Smith, and Honeycrisp, keep their shape better than others. This dish goes well with pork, but it's also sweet enough to be served as an unconventionally savoury dessert.

1   Combine the birch and maple syrups, vinegar, and cinnamon sticks in a pot and bring to a boil over high heat. Cook until the volume has reduced by about half, about 10 minutes. Remove the pan from the heat.

2   Leave the apples whole, or cut them in half and remove the seeds and sharp parts of the core with a paring knife (they'll cook faster halved). Place the apples in the pot and roll them around in the liquid to ensure they are well coated. Cover the pot with a lid and cook over medium heat, rolling the apples around every 5 minutes, until soft, like a ripe pear, and easy to cut with a spoon but not so cooked that they start to split their skin and dissolve. (Different varieties of apples will require different cooking times, so just keep an eye on them and cook until soft but not falling apart. In general, halved apples will cook in 10 to 15 minutes; whole in 20 to 25.) Remove the pan from the heat.

3   Uncover the apples, and let cool until warm, about 15 minutes. Place the warm apples in one large bowl to serve family-style or divide them into individual serving bowls. Drizzle with the cooking liquid. Sprinkle with the finely shredded fresh mint and dust with mushroom powder.

1 cup / 250 mL pure birch syrup

1 cup / 250 mL pure maple syrup

1 cup / 250 mL sherry vinegar

2 x 3-inch / 7.5-cm cinnamon sticks

6 apples (Ambrosia, Granny Smith, or Honeycrisp), unpeeled, whole or halved

8 fresh mint leaves, rolled tightly together and finely cut into ribbons

1 tbsp / 15 mL porcini powder

# THREE SISTERS SOUP

MAKES 6 SERVINGS

Squash, corn, and beans have long been known as the "three sisters" in Indigenous communities. In gardening terms, they are companion plants, supporting and nurturing one another as they grow. The corn shoots skyward, providing a natural pole for the beans to follow as they climb. As they do, they provide some extra support to keep the corn upright. The squash grows low, controlling weeds and keeping the sun off the soil to prevent unnecessary moisture loss. Nutritionally, they provide a combination of protein (beans), carbohydrates (corn and squash), and vitamins. The squash even provide a small amount of fat in the oil contained in their seeds. The three companions also happen to taste great together.

¾ cup / 175 mL dried white beans (navy, great northern, or white kidney / cannellini beans; yields about 1½ cups / 375 mL cooked)

8 cups / 2 L water, plus more for soaking

6 cloves garlic, crushed, divided

½ tsp / 2.5 mL salt, or more to taste

1 medium spaghetti squash (about 2 lbs / 900 g)

½ tsp / 2.5 mL salt and freshly ground black pepper

¼ tsp / 1 mL ground allspice

¼ tsp / 1 mL ground cinnamon

2 tbsp / 30 mL neutral-flavoured cooking oil (such as canola), for frying

½ white onion, finely diced

1 medium carrot, finely diced

1 rib celery, finely diced

¾ cup / 175 mL corn kernels (fresh or frozen)

6 cups / 1.5 L Pheasant Broth (recipe page 280) or good-quality chicken broth

6 sprigs fresh thyme

18 cherry tomatoes, halved

1 tbsp / 15 mL cold-pressed canola oil, for drizzling

2 tbsp / 30 mL finely chopped fresh green herbs of your choice, for garnish

1   Place the beans in a large pot and cover in cold water. Let soak overnight. (If you forget to do this, pour boiling water over the beans and let soak for an hour or so, and then proceed with this recipe.) Drain and then rinse under cold running water.  >>

>>

2   In a 3 to 4 quart / 3 to 4 L soup pot, combine the soaked beans, 3 cloves of crushed garlic, and enough water to cover the beans by 2 inches / 5 cm or so. Bring to a boil over high heat. Cover the pot with a lid, reduce the heat, and simmer for 45 minutes to an hour, until the beans are tender but still retain their shape. Stir in the salt and cook for a few more minutes. Remove the pot from the heat. Using a slotted spoon, transfer the beans to a bowl and keep warm. Discard the garlic. Reserve the cooking liquid.

3   Preheat the oven to 350°F / 180°C (see Tip).

4   Trim off the ends of the squash, and then cut the squash in half lengthwise and scoop out the seeds. Season the cut sides with the salt, pepper, allspice, and cinnamon. Place on a baking sheet cut-side down and bake for about 30 minutes, until the squash is tender. Remove from the oven and let cool slightly. Using the tines of a fork, shred the squash into long strands. Transfer to a bowl, cover, and keep warm.

5   In a skillet over medium-high heat, heat the oil until it shimmers. Reduce the heat to medium and add the onions, carrot, and celery. Cook for 8 to 10 minutes, stirring occasionally, until the onions are soft and translucent and the mixture is fragrant. Add the corn and cook for another 5 minutes, until warmed through. Remove the pan from the heat, cover, and keep warm.

6   In a soup pot, combine the broth and 2 cups / 500 mL of the reserved cooking liquid from the beans (if you don't have enough cooking liquid, simply top it up with water). Add the remaining 3 cloves of garlic and the fresh thyme. Simmer for about 10 minutes, and then discard the garlic and thyme. Taste and adjust the seasoning, if needed.

7   To serve, divide the following into each of 6 bowls: ¼ cup / 60 mL warm beans; ¼ cup / 60 mL warm spaghetti squash; ⅓ cup / 80 mL warm onion, carrot, celery, and corn mixture; 1½ cups / 375 mL hot broth; and 6 tomato halves. Drizzle each serving with the cold-pressed oil. Garnish with any greens or fresh herbs you like, from sprouts to shredded basil or parsley.

---

**TIP**

If you are using a conventional oven, you may need to either cook the squash a little longer or increase the oven temperature by 25°F / 4°C.

---

# BISON LIVER AND PARSLEY SOUP

MAKES 8 TO 10 SERVINGS

Bison graze naturally on grassy pasture throughout their life right up until slaughter. This gives their meat a slightly less fat-marbled profile than beef, but it's also healthier. The nutrient profile both for their meat and liver is outstanding. Liver isn't for everyone, but bison liver tends to be milder in flavour than beef liver. Soaking it in milk also eliminates much of the stronger taste that puts most people off.

1½ lb / 680 g bison liver (about half of a medium-size bison liver), rinsed and patted dry with a clean cloth or paper towel

2 cups / 500 mL milk (approx.)

¾ cup / 175 mL canola oil, divided

3 cups / 750 mL carrots, cut into 1-inch / 2.5-cm dice

3 cups / 750 mL celery ribs, cut into 1-inch / 2.5-cm dice

3 cups / 750 mL diced onion

4 cups / 1 L all-purpose flour

2 tbsp / 30 mL salt, plus extra as needed

2 tbsp / 30 mL freshly ground black pepper, plus extra as needed

8 cups / 2 L Bison Bone Broth (recipe page 276)

1 lemon, juiced

3 cups / 750 mL corn kernels (fresh or frozen)

6 cloves garlic

4 sprigs fresh rosemary

10 to 12 sprigs fresh thyme

1 tbsp / 15 mL whole black peppercorns

1 dried bay leaf

1½ tsp / 7 mL red pepper flakes

1 large bunch flat-leaf parsley, stems removed, roughly chopped

1   Using a sharp knife, cut the liver into 1-inch / 2.5-cm cubes. Transfer to a bowl and pour over enough milk to cover. Soak for an hour or two.

2   Pour ¼ cup / 60 mL of the canola oil into a large soup pot or Dutch oven over medium heat. Cook the carrots, stirring occasionally, just until they start to soften, about 8 minutes, then add the celery and onion and cook for another 10 minutes, until the onions are soft and translucent. Set aside. >>

3    Combine the flour, salt, and pepper in a shallow dish. Working in batches, dredge the liver cubes in the flour mixture until well coated. Shake off excess flour.

4    Pour the remaining ½ cup / 125 mL of canola oil in a heavy skillet and set over medium-high heat. Add the floured liver cubes and sear for about 1 minute per side, until browned all over. Transfer the browned liver to the soup pot with the vegetables. Add the broth along with the lemon juice, corn, garlic, rosemary, thyme, peppercorns, bay leaf, and red pepper flakes. Season with salt and pepper, to taste.

5    Bring the soup to a simmer over medium heat. Reduce the heat to low, add the parsley, and cook, covered, for 30 to 45 minutes, or until the liver is just tender. Serve hot in bowls, with a slice of bread or bannock, if you wish.

# SMOKED NORTHERN PIKE WITH BARLEY, WILD RICE, AND KALE SALAD

MAKES 2 TO 4 SERVINGS

Northern pike (*Esox lucius*) is an abundant and delicious freshwater fish found in Canada and the northern United States. They're often gliding around stands of cattails and reeds in murky water, or cruising the shallows of Prairie lakes. In Canada, they're also found in deep mountain lakes and cold northern lakes. They're an ugly-looking fish, with a bone structure that makes them a bit tricky to fillet, but the flesh is firm and delicious. The nice thing about smoked northern pike is that the remaining bones are easier to find and remove than in a fresh fillet.

## FOR THE SALAD

¼ cup / 60 mL pearl barley, rinsed and drained

¾ cup / 175 mL Pheasant Broth (recipe page 280) or good-quality chicken broth

½ tsp / 2.5 mL salt

½ cup / 125 mL wild rice, rinsed and drained

1½ cups / 375 mL water or Pheasant Broth (recipe page 280) or good-quality chicken broth

2 oz / 55 g raw kale (about 3 leaves)

## FOR THE VINAIGRETTE

½ cup / 125 mL apple cider vinegar

2 tbsp / 30 mL pure maple syrup

1 tbsp / 15 mL Minced Garlic and Shallots in Oil (recipe page 282)

2 tbsp / 30 mL cold-pressed canola oil

2 tbsp / 30 mL finely chopped fresh parsley leaves

¼ tsp / 1 mL sea salt, or to taste

## FOR THE PIKE

1 x 3-oz / 85-g smoked northern pike fillet

2 to 4 tbsp / 30 to 60 mL golden caviar, for garnish

1  *Make the salad:* Toast the barley in a dry cast iron skillet on medium heat for about 10 minutes, until it's pale golden and fragrant. Add the ¾ cup / 75 mL pheasant broth and salt, and bring to a simmer, stirring occasionally. Check for doneness at about 30 minutes: You want it to be cooked al dente—fully cooked through the grain but still firm. Remove the pan from the heat and set aside to cool. Strain any excess liquid.

2    Meanwhile, combine the wild rice and 1 ½ cups / 375 mL water or broth in a small pot (if you use water, add a pinch of salt). Bring it to a boil, stir, reduce the heat to medium, cover, and simmer for 45 minutes, until the rice has opened up. Remove the pan from the heat, strain any excess liquid, and set aside.

3    Remove the kale ribs and tear the leaves into bite-size pieces. Place them in a large bowl along with the cooked barley and wild rice.

4    *Make the vinaigrette:* In a jar, combine the cider vinegar, maple syrup, garlic shallot mix, oil, parsley, and salt. Shake well, until emulsified. Pour over the salad and stir until well coated.

5    Remove the skin of the smoked pike with your fingers. Cut the flesh into 3 or 4 strips. Spread the salad on a platter and place the pieces of northern pike on top. Finish with golden caviar. Serve immediately.

# BISON-BROTH POACHED HALIBUT WITH GRILLED CABBAGE, WHIPPED POTATOES, BAKED KALE, AND ROASTED BEECH MUSHROOMS

MAKES 4 SERVINGS | SPECIAL EQUIPMENT: POTATO RICER

It must be obvious by the number of times fried kale pops up in my recipes that I absolutely love it. But how about grilled cabbage? And sweet mustard seed compote? It's always interesting to combine members of the Brassica family. They grow so well on the Canadian Prairies and, being cousins, the flavours pair well with each other, too.

Halibut is a bit of a splurge and should only be bought from a reputable fishmonger. You only need a little — the other elements of this dish do the heavy lifting.

### FOR THE WHIPPED POTATOES

4 Yukon Gold potatoes

Salt, to taste

2 tbsp / 30 mL unsalted butter

¼ cup / 60 mL whipping (35%) cream

### FOR THE STEAMED BEECH MUSHROOMS

5 oz / 140 g beech (shimeji) mushrooms (brown or white)

1 tbsp / 15 mL Minced Garlic and Shallots in Oil (recipe page 282)

Pinch of salt

### FOR THE GRILLED CABBAGE LEAVES

4 to 8 green cabbage leaves

1 tsp / 5 mL canola or olive oil

Fleur de sel, to taste

### FOR THE BAKED KALE

2 bunches kale (about 14 oz / 400 g), centre ribs removed and leaves torn into bite-size pieces

2 tbsp / 30 mL canola or olive oil

Fleur de sel, to taste

### FOR THE POACHED HALIBUT

1 × 2-lb / 900-g halibut fillet, skin off and pinboned

4 cups / 1 L Bison Bone Broth (recipe page 276)

5 sprigs fresh thyme

2 cloves garlic

1 sprig fresh rosemary

4 tsp / 20 mL Sweet Mustard Seed Compote (recipe page 283)

½ bunch fresh parsley leaves, finely chopped

1   Preheat the oven to 350°F / 180°C (see Tip).

2   *Make the whipped potatoes:* Peel and quarter the potatoes. Put them in a pot with enough water to cover and add a pinch of salt. Bring the water to a boil, reduce the heat, and simmer until the potatoes are tender, 10 to 20 minutes. Drain and set aside to air dry. Once dry, put them through a potato ricer. If you don't have a ricer, mash them well with a potato masher until smooth and fluffy. Add the riced potatoes to the bowl of a stand mixer along with the butter, cream, and salt. Using the whisk attachment, mix on low speed for about 20 to 30 seconds (they should remain fluffy if you don't overmix). Cover and keep warm.

3   *Steam the mushrooms:* Break the mushroom cluster into 4 even portions and place in the centre of a 12- by 12-inch / 30- by 30-cm piece of aluminum foil. Add the garlic shallot mix and a pinch of salt. Seal the package tightly. Place in the preheated oven and cook for about 15 minutes, until the mushrooms are soft and glossy.

4   *Grill the cabbage:* Preheat the grill to medium (350°F / 180°C). Run a rolling pin over the cabbage leaves a few times on each side to tenderize them, and then brush both sides with oil. Place the cabbage directly onto the grill, and cook for about 15 seconds per side, flipping once they're char-marked (they should be soft and flexible). Remove from grill and season with a generous amount of fleur de sel. Cut the leaves into quarters and set aside.

5   *Bake the kale:* Increase the oven temperature to 400°F / 200°C (see Tip). Line two large baking sheets in parchment paper. Place the kale pieces in a large bowl. Add the oil and toss until the leaves are well coated. Arrange the leaves in a single layer on the prepared baking sheets. (It's okay to crowd the kale on the sheets when they go in the oven. The pieces will shrink as they bake.) Cook for 10 to 15 minutes, stirring every 5 minutes, until golden brown around the edges but soft in the middle. Season with a pinch of fleur de sel and set aside.

6   *Poach the halibut:* Cut the fish into 4 even pieces and set aside. Bring the bone broth to a boil in a braising skillet, and then reduce the heat to low. Add the fish, thyme, garlic, and rosemary. Cover with a tight-fitting lid or foil and simmer gently for 10 minutes, until the halibut is firm and cooked through to the centre (the flesh should be opaque).

7   *Assemble the dish:* Place a generous scoop of whipped potatoes on each serving plate, and then arrange the halibut at an angle on the whipped potatoes. Top with about 1 tsp / 5 mL sweet mustard compote and a pinch of chopped parsley. Add some mushrooms, grilled cabbage, and a handful of kale to each plate. Serve immediately.

---
**TIP**

If you are using a conventional oven, you may need to either cook the items a little longer or increase the oven temperatures by 25°F / 4°C.

# ON CREATIVITY AND INSPIRATION

**IF YOU CHALLENGE ME** with crazy ideas and thoughts, that's when I come up with my best work. Often, I dream up dishes in the kitchen with my staff. I'll say, "Today the emotion is a running creek. How are we going to make something that evokes a running creek?" Then we figure it out. That's the luxury of cooking in a professional restaurant.

I travel a lot for inspiration as well. I go to Chicago to eat. Same with New York, Toronto, Calgary, and Vancouver. I'm also very inspired by the chefs in my hometown. I went to high school with Blair Lebsack, chef and co-owner of RGE RD restaurant. Blair's food is about a connection to the land, and he does it so well. He understands his ingredients, like a good chef should.

My favourite restaurant in Edmonton is Bar Bricco or any of Daniel Costa's three restaurants, really. Daniel is Italian-Canadian. He has family in Italy. He makes delicious food based on his family's heritage and traditions. It's so strong and clear — and that's one of the reasons he's the city's best chef, and one of the best in Canada.

My world is exactly the opposite: I don't have that original connection to my family's history, to my ancestors. I don't have the same information. Like it is for many in my community, those connections were destroyed, outlawed, and disrupted in every way. I have to figure out so much on my own, and it's slow and frustrating work. I have to piece it together by listening to stories, by taking in what the

A prep station, complete with a stone and clay oven, for an outdoor cooking and dining event.

Chiefs and Elders are saying, and by travelling to meet other Indigenous people and gathering from them whatever information they can offer me. That's the hard part about the Indigenous world in which I live. If you are cooking French food, you just have to follow the instructions. Maybe you put your own twist on it, but you have a foundation of key recipes to draw on. My food has to come from stories. Nothing's really written down.

So much knowledge has been destroyed — that's why I'm working so hard to learn all I can, not just about my Plains Cree culture but also Indigenous cooking and ingredients across Canada. I lost a lot of time early in life not knowing where I came from when I could have spent it learning. I have a lot to catch up on.

*"I'll say, 'Today the emotion is a running creek. How are we going to make something that evokes a running creek?' Then we figure it out."*

# BEET-CURED SALMON WITH CHANTERELLES AND SASKATOON SAUCE

MAKES 4 TO 6 SERVINGS

King salmon (also known as Chinook salmon and spring salmon) and saskatoon berries are two of the four "food chiefs" for the Syilx (Okanagan) people, who live in the interior of British Columbia. From what I have learned about the Syilx tradition, the Creator sent Coyote to tell the elements, animals, and plants that people were coming. The four food chiefs — Black Bear, King Salmon, Saskatoon Berries, and Bitterroot — assembled and decided on a plan to feed the people-to-be. And that is how food was given to the Syilx.

I have family in the Shuswap region (Syilx territory), and I love spending time in the Okanagan. There's really good mushroom foraging in this area, too. All these things came together for me in this recipe.

Plan to start this recipe a day ahead.

### FOR THE BEET-CURED SALMON

1 cup / 250 mL granulated sugar

½ cup / 125 mL salt

1 × 3.3-lb / 1.5-kg sashimi-grade King salmon, skin on and pinboned

1 cup / 250 mL fresh beet juice (from about 4 large red beets)

### FOR THE MUSHROOMS

¼ cup / 60 mL canola oil

4 large shallots, finely diced

4 cups / 1 L chanterelle mushrooms, roughly chopped

Salt, to taste

### FOR THE SASKATOON BERRY SAUCE

1½ cups / 375 mL saskatoon berries

3 bay leaves (fresh or dried)

3 x 3-inch / 7.5-cm cinnamon sticks

3 tbsp / 45 mL granulated sugar

### FOR SERVING

1½ tbsp / 22 mL cold-pressed flax oil, to finish

Several dill fronds

Salt, to taste

1   *Make the beet-cured salmon:* Combine the sugar and salt in a bowl. Place the fillet on a shallow baking dish or rimmed baking sheet and cover both sides in the sugar mixture. Pour the beet juice evenly over the fillet. Cover loosely with plastic wrap and refrigerate for 24 hours. >>

2   *Prepare the mushrooms:* Heat the oil in a pan over medium-high heat. Add the shallots, mushrooms, and salt (the mushrooms and shallots will sizzle at first but will calm down). Cook until very soft, about 8 minutes, stirring occasionally. Remove the pan from the heat and let cool slightly.

3   *Make the saskatoon berry sauce:* Combine the berries, bay leaves, cinnamon sticks, and sugar in a small pan. Cook over medium-high heat, stirring occasionally, until the berries burst and the mixture has reduced in volume by a quarter. Taste and add more sugar, if needed. Discard the bay leaves and cinnamon sticks. Remove the pan from the heat and set the sauce aside.

4   *Cook the salmon:* Take the salmon out of its cure and rinse well under cool running water, then pat dry with a clean cloth or paper towel. Using a sharp knife, cut the salmon into thin slices against the grain.

5   *Assemble the dish:* Smear a spoonful of saskatoon berry sauce on each serving plate. Place a spoonful of the mushroom purée near it. Arrange the fish on top of the mushroom purée. Drizzle with the flax oil, and sprinkle with dill fronds and a pinch of salt. Serve immediately.

# COLD-SMOKED HAIDA GWAII SABLEFISH WITH SWEET MUSTARD COMPOTE, SASKATOON BERRIES, AND BEET TOPS

MAKES 4 TO 8 SERVINGS

Haida Gwaii is a collection of hundreds of islands off the northern coast of British Columbia. The Haida are expert carvers and have a beautiful and distinctive artistic aesthetic. I have two Haida-inspired tattoos, an eagle and a bear, on my chest.

The islands and the sea in Haida Gwaii are incredibly pristine and beautiful. I buy seafood from Haida Wild Seafoods on Graham Island. They buy directly from responsible and sustainable fishers. Their smoked sablefish is one of my favourite products.

1   Peel the cucumber and cut the onion crosswise in half (into two quarter pieces). Using a mandoline slicer on the thinnest setting or your precision knife skills, cut the red onion and cucumber into very thin slices, about ⅛-inch / 3-mm thick. Place in a large bowl, along with the capers, parsley, and sweet mustard compote, and set aside.

2   Using a very sharp knife, working against the grain, cut the sablefish on an angle into very thin slices, as if you were cutting gravlax or thin pieces of smoked salmon. Add to the bowl and gently mix until the compote "dresses" the other components. Cover and refrigerate.

3   Bring a large pot of salted water to a boil. Prepare an ice water bath (a large bowl filled with cold water and ice cubes). Place the beet tops in the boiling water and cook for 2 to 3 minutes, until the leaves and stems are softly wilted. Using a wire-mesh scoop or slotted spoon, transfer the beet tops to the ice water bath for a couple of minutes and then lay them out on a clean cloth or paper towel. >>

1 small (baby) English cucumber

½ red onion

1 tbsp / 15 mL capers, rinsed and drained

2 tbsp / 30 mL roughly chopped fresh parsley

2 tbsp / 30 mL Sweet Mustard Seed Compote (recipe page 283)

½ loin smoked sablefish

3 beets, tops only

30 saskatoon or mossberries, for garnish

Fleur de sel

4    To serve, arrange the beet tops in a neat line along the long edge of a cutting board. Sprinkle the saskatoon berries evenly along the beet tops. Parallel to the beet tops, arrange the sablefish mixture in a line. Finish by sprinkling everything with a pinch of fleur de sel. Serve chilled.

# LEEK-ASH-COATED ARCTIC CHAR WITH BLACK GARLIC MUSHROOMS AND SQUASH PURÉE

MAKES 6 TO 8 SERVINGS

I want you to eat this with your hands! It's a shore lunch, and it should be as if you just caught the fish (maybe you did if you're lucky enough to fish in Canada's north) and you don't really want to wash up afterward. The leek ash stands in for the campfire that you'd be cooking this on. The ash gets on the fish. Guess what? The slightly bitter ash is delicious with the fatty flesh and crispy skin of the Arctic char as well as the sweetness of the butternut squash purée.

## FOR THE SQUASH PURÉE

1 medium butternut squash (about 2 lbs / 900 g)

2 tbsp / 30 mL canola oil

1½ cups / 375 mL Pheasant Broth (recipe page 280) or good-quality chicken broth

1 tbsp / 15 mL Minced Garlic and Shallots in Oil (recipe page 282)

¼ cup / 60 mL butter

Salt and freshly ground black pepper, to taste

## FOR THE BLACK GARLIC MUSHROOMS

1 cup / 250 mL assorted mushrooms, sliced

2 tbsp / 30 mL finely minced black garlic (see sidebar)

1 tsp / 5 mL minced garlic

2 tbsp / 30 mL butter

¼ cup + 2 tbsp (90 mL) Bison Bone Broth (recipe page 276), chicken broth, or vegetable broth

½ tsp / 2.5 mL sea salt

¼ tsp / 1 mL freshly ground black pepper

## FOR THE LEEK-ASH-COATED CHAR

2 leeks

1 cup / 250 mL pickling spice (see Tip)

2 cups + 2 tbsp / 530 mL canola oil, divided

1 cup / 250 mL fresh curly parsley, leaves only

Pinch of fleur de sel

2 x 2-lb / 900-g Arctic char fillets, skin on and pinboned

3 tbsp / 45 mL Puffed Fried Rice, for garnish (optional; recipe page 285)

**BLACK GARLIC** is whole-bulb garlic that is aged through a prolonged application of heat and constant humidity. The garlic cloves turn black, soft, and sticky. They also develop an interesting tang, reminiscent of tamarind paste or reduced balsamic vinegar. Once only available in Asian grocery stores, they can now be found at specialty grocers and online.

1   *Make the squash purée:* Preheat the oven to 375°F / 190°C (see Tip on page 166). Line a baking sheet in parchment paper.

2   Using the tip of a sharp knife, pierce holes all over the squash. Place it on the prepared baking sheet. Using a pastry brush, cover the rind in oil. Bake in the preheated oven for 1 hour, turning it over after 30 minutes (it's cooked when you can easily pierce the rind and flesh with a knife and the shape has sunken in somewhat). Remove from the oven and let cool.

3   Cut the cooled squash in half, lengthwise. Using a spoon, scoop out and discard the seeds and strings. Scoop the flesh from the rind and place the flesh in a blender or food processor (discard the rind). Warm the broth in a small pot on the stove and then add it to the blender along with the garlic shallot mix and butter. Blend until smooth. Season with salt and pepper.

4   *Make the mushrooms:* Combine the sliced mushrooms, black garlic, regular garlic, and butter in a saucepan over medium heat. Cook until the mushrooms are soft and most of the liquid has cooked off, about 5 minutes. Transfer the mixture to a blender or food processor. Add the broth, salt, and pepper. Blend to a thick paste (add a bit of butter or more broth to loosen the mixture, if needed). Set aside.

5   *Prepare the char:* Preheat the grill to medium (375°F / 190°C). Trim both ends of the leeks, leaving lots of the green parts on. Cut in half lengthwise, and then cut lengthwise again, and then once more to make long, thin ribbons. Place the leeks on a length of aluminum foil and transfer the foil to the hot grill. Close the lid and grill, checking regularly, until the leeks turn to black ash, about 30 minutes. Remove from the grill and set aside (foil and ash together). When cool enough to handle, use a rolling pin to crush and crumble the blackened leeks into a coarse powder.

6   In a small dry saucepan, toast the pickling spices over low heat, shaking the pan a few times to prevent burning, for 5 to 10 minutes or until fragrant. Remove the pan from the heat and transfer the toasted spices to a plate. Set aside to cool. Combine with the leek ash in a blender and pulse to a coarse grind.

7   In a small pot, heat 2 cups / 500 mL of the canola oil to 350°F / 180°C. Deep-fry the parsley leaves until golden brown, 2 to 3 minutes. Using a wire-mesh scoop or slotted spoon, transfer the fried parsley to paper towel. Season with fleur de sel and set aside.

8   Preheat a grill to medium (375°F / 190°C). Coat both sides of the char generously in the leek-ash and spice powder, and then brush with the remaining 2 tbsp / 30 mL oil. Place the prepared char skin-side down on the grill (don't worry, char has a good layer of fat to deal with intense heat on the skin). Grill until the skin is very crispy and the fish is cooked through, 5 or 6 minutes (the flesh should be opaque in the centre; cook time will depend on the thickness of the fillets). Alternatively, cook the char in a cast iron pan on the stove: Heat 1½ tbsp / 22 mL of oil and cook char skin-side down for 4 minutes, then flip and cook for 2 to 3 minutes. >>

9   *Assemble the dish:* Place the grilled fish on a platter. Spoon the mushrooms and squash purée around the fish. Garnish the squash with some puffed fried rice, if using. Sprinkle everything with the deep-fried parsley. Serve immediately—and encourage your guests to eat with their hands.

---

### TIPS

If you have a good pickling spice that you like, by all means use it. The pickling spice I use contains coriander seed, mustard seed, crushed bay leaves, dill seed, fenugreek, broken cinnamon quills, ginger, allspice, crushed red pepper, black peppercorn, and cloves. All these items combine to impart the fish with a delicious flavour that your guests will love but have a hard time identifying.

---

If you are using a conventional oven, you may need to either cook the squash a little longer or increase the oven temperature by 25°F / 4°C.

---

## WILD RICE

*Zizania palustris* and *Zizania aquatica* are two species of wild rice native to Canada and the United States. Interestingly, neither are true rice but rather freshwater grasses (found around the edges of lakes and in slow-flowing streams) with an edible seed that is harvested in early fall. Wild rice has the distinction of being Canada's only indigenous cereal crop. Almost three-quarters of the total amount of wild rice grown in Canada comes from Saskatchewan. The rest is produced in Manitoba, Ontario, and Alberta (in that order). It features a long brownish-black husk that, when cooked, splits to reveal the white inside. Very high in protein, it has a lovely chewy texture and nutty, smoky flavour. In general, 1 cup (250 mL) of uncooked wild rice will yield 3 cups (750 mL) of cooked rice. Cooking time can be anywhere from 45 minutes to an hour (or more if you want the kernels fully opened and soft). Add cooked wild rice to soups or enjoy it cold in salads. Of course, it's great served simply as a side dish or quickly fried in hot oil and then generously salted (see Puffed Fried Rice, page 285).

# HONEY-BRINED ROAST PHEASANT
# WITH ACORN SQUASH AND FRESH SAGE

MAKES 2 SERVINGS | SPECIAL EQUIPMENT: LARGE STOCKPOT OR 8-QUART / 7.5-L FOOD-SAFE
CONTAINER; ROASTING PAN

Pheasants are not native to North America — they were introduced from Asia in the early 1800s — but they're now so common that they are part of the game bird category for hunting. They range in weight from 2 to 4 lbs / 900 g to 1.8 kg and are really tasty when roasted. Pheasants are normally hunted in the fall because they're fattening up for winter, which is also when winter squash, like acorn squash, is in season. Unsurprisingly, the two make a great pairing. Once you've served this dish, reserve the pheasant carcass and extra bits to make Pheasant Broth (recipe page 280), a delicious alternative to chicken broth.

### FOR THE BRINE

8 cups / 2 L water

½ cup / 125 mL coarse kosher salt

¼ cup / 60 mL good-quality organic honey (see page 134)

8 cloves garlic, peeled and crushed, divided

2 tbsp / 30 mL whole black peppercorns

1 lemon, halved

### FOR THE PHEASANT

1 pheasant, plucked and cleaned

Several sprigs of fresh sage, rosemary, and thyme

Salt and freshly ground black pepper, to taste

### FOR THE ACORN SQUASH

1 medium acorn squash

1 tbsp / 15 mL canola oil

Salt and freshly ground black pepper, to taste

¼ tsp / 1 mL rubbed sage

3 large kale leaves, for garnish (optional)

Pea shoots, for garnish (optional)

1   In a large stockpot or an 8-quart / 7.5-L food-safe container, bring the water, salt, honey, 4 cloves of the garlic, peppercorns, and lemon halves to a boil. Stir and cover. Remove from the heat and set aside to cool completely.

2   Once the brine is cool, put the pheasant into the brine. Cover and refrigerate for at least 4 hours, or overnight. >>

>>

3   Preheat the oven to 400°F / 200°C (see Tip). Line a
    baking sheet in parchment paper.

4   Drive the tip of a long, sharp knife into the squash
    and carefully push down to cut it lengthwise in half.
    Using a spoon, scoop out the seeds and discard.
    Brush the inside of the squash with oil and season
    with salt, pepper, and rubbed sage. Place cut-side up
    on the prepared baking sheet. Set aside.

5   Remove the pheasant from the brine and pat dry
    with paper towel (discard brine). Stuff the cavity with
    the fresh herbs and the remaining 4 garlic cloves.
    Rub generous amounts of salt and pepper all over
    the skin. Place the pheasant in a roasting pan and
    put on the lowest rack in the preheated oven. Put
    the squash on the rack above. Reduce the heat to
    350°F / 180°C and roast both for 30 to 40 minutes:
    The squash flesh should be golden brown and soft;
    the internal temperature of the pheasant should reach
    165°F / 72°C. Remove the pans from the oven and let
    the pheasant rest for about 10 minutes.

6   Carve the pheasant and arrange on a platter with the
    roasted squash halves, or leave the pheasant whole
    and carve at the table. If you like, place the pheasant
    on a few leaves of kale to help the bird sit more
    firmly on the platter. Garnish the squash with fresh
    pea shoots, if you wish.

---

**TIP**

If you are using a conventional oven, you
may need to either cook the dish a little
longer or increase the oven temperature
by 25°F / 4°C.

---

# PAN-SEARED DUCK BREAST WITH CREAMED CABBAGE, BLACKENED CORN, AND "CONFIT" CARROTS

MAKES 4 SERVINGS

When I was a young man, my dad used to take me and my cousins duck hunting. When we came home with our birds, my mom was responsible for plucking and cleaning them. We ate all kinds of wild meat, but duck was important to our family table. This recipe is a tribute to what my family knew as good food and contains the flavours of fall from our fields and garden. I cherish the memories we made foraging for great meals over the years.

1   Place the carrots in a small soup pot, and pour over enough oil to just cover them. Heat the oil to 175°F/80°C. Cook the carrots gently until fork-tender, about 45 minutes.

2   Meanwhile, using a sharp knife, lightly score the duck skin, cutting into the fat (but not the meat) in a crisscross pattern (this will help the duck fat cook evenly, and also drain some of the fat).

3   Season the breasts with salt, pepper, and sage. Let sit at room temperature for about 30 minutes.

4   Preheat the grill to 350°F/180°C. Preheat the oven to 350°F/180°C (see Tip on page 172).

5   Brush the corn with oil and season with salt and pepper. Grill the corn, rotating until lightly charred.

6   Transfer to a platter. Tent loosely with aluminum foil to keep warm. >>

2 medium carrots, cut into 1-inch/2.5-cm pieces

1¼ cup/310 mL (or more) neutral-flavoured cooking oil (such as canola)

4 duck breasts, skin on

Salt and freshly ground black pepper, to taste

1 tbsp/15 mL rubbed sage

2 cobs of corn, husked, halved

½ small head green Savoy cabbage, thinly sliced

8 large cloves garlic, crushed

1 cup/250 mL whipping (35%) cream, plus extra if needed

½ cup/125 mL dry white wine

Salt and freshly ground black pepper, to taste

24 pea shoots (approx.), for garnish (optional)

7   In a heavy skillet, heat about ¼ cup / 60 mL canola oil over medium heat. Add the cabbage and garlic, and sauté until the cabbage is soft but not coloured. Stir in the cream and wine. Cook until the cabbage is soft enough to blend. Using an immersion blender, blend the mixture in the pan until smooth (or transfer to a blender), adding more cream and wine as required to loosen. Season with salt and pepper. Cover and keep warm.

8   Add another ¼ cup / 60 mL canola oil to a cast iron or oven-safe skillet over medium heat and heat until it shimmers. Sear the duck, skin-side down, for 5 or 6 minutes, until the skin is golden and the fat has rendered off. Turn the breasts over and sear the other side for 2 minutes. Place the pan in the preheated oven to finish cooking, 6 to 8 minutes for medium-rare.

9   Remove the pan from the oven and transfer the cooked breasts to a cutting board with a trough, tent loosely with foil, and let rest for a few minutes.

10  To serve, pour a few tablespoons of warm cabbage cream sauce on each plate. Carefully arrange a few pieces of confit carrots around the outside. Place a half corn cob per plate. Using a sharp knife, slice the duck breast against the grain into ½-inch / 1-cm slices. Fan out one breast per plate on top of the cabbage cream. Scatter about 6 pea shoots on each plate.

---
**TIP**

If you are using a conventional oven, you may need to either cook the dish a little longer or increase the oven temperature by 25°F / 4°C.

---

# ELK TENDERLOIN WITH GRILLED OYSTER MUSHROOMS

MAKES 2 TO 3 SERVINGS | SPECIAL EQUIPMENT: ROASTING PAN WITH ROASTING RACK

My dad and I go elk hunting in the fall. However, it's the one animal I've never had a chance to shoot because Dad always gets one before I do. When we hunt together, we go in opposite directions, in a type of circle. And every time, Dad gets the shot. It's such a large animal that yields so much meat, you only need to shoot one. The herb bundles are really just a decorative garnish, but they remind me of a bundle of herbs used in a smudge ceremony.

1   Take the tenderloin out of the refrigerator about an hour before cooking and cover loosely with aluminum foil to bring it to room temperature.

2   Preheat the oven to 350°F / 180°C (see Tip on page 128).

3   In a bowl, combine the oil and chopped parsley, adding a bit more oil if needed to make a sticky paste. Using your hands, press it firmly onto the tenderloin, adhering as much of it as possible. Place the tenderloin on a wire rack set in a roasting pan. Set aside.

4   In a small bowl, combine the oil and garlic shallot mix. Gently toss the mushroom clusters in the mixture until well coated. Place the seasoned mushrooms stem-side down on a baking sheet.

5   Place the mushrooms on the top rack in the oven. Place the tenderloin on the rack below. Cook both in the preheated oven for 10 to 12 minutes, or until the mushrooms are slightly soft and start to give up their water and the tenderloin reaches an internal temperature of 135°F / 57°C (for medium-rare). Remove the pans from the oven, tent loosely with aluminum foil, and let the tenderloin rest for about 10 minutes. >>

1 x 2-lb / 900-g elk tenderloin

1 tbsp / 15 mL canola oil

¾ cup / 175 mL finely chopped fresh parsley leaves

½ cup / 125 mL canola oil

2 tbsp / 30 mL Minced Garlic and Shallots in Oil (recipe page 282)

4 bundles pink oyster mushrooms (about a handful each)

A few sprigs each fresh rosemary, thyme, and sage

2 to 3 small bunches of red grapes (preferably red wine grapes)

Salt and freshly ground black pepper, to taste

6   While the mushrooms and elk are cooking, bundle up two or three sprigs of herbs (depending on how many plates you are making) and tie them together with a piece of butcher's twine. Set aside.

7   Once the tenderloin has rested, cut it into 6 even portions. Divide evenly among the serving plates, along with the mushroom clusters. Garnish each with a decorative herb bundle and a small bunch of grapes. Season with salt and pepper, and serve.

---

**TIP**

If you are using a conventional oven, you may need to either cook the dish a little longer or increase the oven temperature by 25°F / 4°C.

---

# CHARCOAL BISON SKIRT STEAK WITH QUICK DILL PICKLES AND SWEET MUSTARD SEED COMPOTE

MAKES 4 SERVINGS

Recipes come to me when I think about what grows together, or even when I think about what the animal I am about to cook eats. This recipe is a good example. Bison range and graze on Prairie grasses. Cold-pressed hemp has that interesting grassy aroma and flavour. And nowadays the farmlands of the Prairies are covered in fields of yellow canola, which is from the family of mustards known as Brassicaceae. The canola and mustard fields are highly dependent on the work of bees, so I wanted the taste of honey in this dish as well. To balance the sweetness, I included apple cider vinegar. As for the quick dill pickles, this is a tribute to my mom — in summer, the house always smelled of pickles and brining liquids. No one makes better pickles than my mom.

FOR THE BISON SKIRT STEAK

1 × 2.2-lb/1-kg bison skirt steak

½ cup/125 mL cold-pressed hemp oil

½ cup/125 mL canola oil

½ cup/125 mL apple cider vinegar

1 tsp/5 mL salt

1 tsp/5 mL freshly ground black pepper

1 cup/250 mL minced shallots

½ cup/125 mL minced garlic

½ cup/125 mL roughly chopped flat-leaf parsley leaves

Fleur de sel

FOR THE QUICK PICKLES

2 cups/500 mL apple cider vinegar

2 cups/500 mL good-quality organic honey (see page 134)

½ cup/125 mL loosely packed fresh dill fronds

1 English cucumber

FOR SERVING

½ cup/125 mL Sweet Mustard Seed Compote (recipe page 285)

1   *Marinate the steak:* Using the tip of a sharp knife, score the top of the skirt steak by making ⅛-inch-/3-mm-deep cuts across the grain every 2 inches/5 cm or so. Then repeat in the other direction, cutting perpendicular to the first cuts. Turn the steak over and repeat this process. >>

>>

2   Combine the hemp oil, canola oil, vinegar, salt, pepper, shallots, and garlic in a resealable bag. Add the steak. Seal, pressing out as much air as possible, and turn to coat the meat. Refrigerate for at least a couple of hours or overnight.

3   *Make the quick pickles:* Combine the apple cider vinegar, honey, and dill in a large soup pot. Bring to a boil, then reduce the heat and simmer until the liquid has reduced by about half, about 15 minutes. Meanwhile, shred the cucumbers with a box grater (as in the photo) or slice them thinly in rounds by knife or with a mandoline. Once the pickling liquid is ready, reduce the heat to low, remove the dill with a slotted spoon, and submerge the cucumber slices. Simmer gently for 5 minutes, no longer. Using tongs, transfer the cucumbers to a jar or heatproof resealable container. Add just enough of the hot pickling liquid to cover the cucumbers. Seal, let cool, and refrigerate for a couple hours or overnight.

4   *Prepare the steak:* About 30 minutes before you want to serve this meal, take the skirt steak out of the fridge and bring it up to room temperature.

5   Preheat the grill to high (550°F / 285°C). When the grill is good and hot—there should be a sizzle when the steak hits it—sear the skirt steak for 3 to 4 minutes only per side (for medium-rare). Be careful not to overcook the steak. Transfer the steak to a cutting board and sprinkle with the chopped parsley and fleur de sel. Tent loosely with aluminum foil and let rest for about 5 minutes.

6   Using a sharp knife, working against the grain, cut the steak on an angle into 1-inch / 2.5-cm slices. To serve, arrange family-style on butcher paper or a platter, along with the pickled cucumbers and the sweet mustard seed compote.

# ON FEAR
# AND ANXIETY

**WHEN THINGS SCARE ME,** I try to figure out why — understanding the root causes of my fears is helpful to me. When I get an anxiety attack, I know I just have to fight through it and keep going. I do this because I know that if I don't do something out of fear or anxiety, I'll regret it later.

Public speaking used to be a big source of anxiety for me. It took me a long time to figure out how to do it well. I've since done a lot of television, but I can still remember my first appearance and being so afraid of screwing up on air or burning something or dropping something that I didn't get any sleep the night before. After a few more appearances, I realized that I just had to speak louder, talk more clearly and precisely, and make sure I had a point. The more public speaking I did, the better I got at it.

I still get really bad anxiety attacks — they started in my early 30s, around the same time I found out about my birth parents and that I was originally from Enoch — but I know now that I can get through the episodes. They pass eventually. And it's important that I get through them because I need to get to where I'm going, despite the uncomfortable feelings that can arise sometimes.

I also know what it feels like to do something that no one expects you can do. And I've certainly had times in my life where I couldn't even meet my own expectations. I know that in the end if I work hard enough and achieve certain things, it's not about me, it's about changing expectations of those around me. In the end, though, I simply focus on bringing people together over food. Take this book for example; it took four years to write. Some people didn't think I'd ever finish. So now that it's finished, it feels like winning a private little war.

# BISON STRIPLOIN WITH CELERIAC CREAM AND APPLE ONION RELISH

MAKES 2 TO 4 SERVINGS

There's a grilled steak culture here on the Canadian Prairies. And we had a big root cellar on our acreage in central Alberta. Bison steak, root vegetables, cream, and apple relish are all familiar flavours of my childhood.

The rosemary brush is not just decorative — each diner will use it to paint the top of their bison steak with the melted butter. It imparts a lovely aroma.

### FOR THE STRIPLOIN

2 to 4 New York strip bison steaks

½ head celeriac (about ½ lb / 225 g), cut into 1-inch / 2.5-cm pieces

1 cup / 250 mL half-and-half (10%) cream

3 tbsp / 45 mL butter

Salt and freshly ground black pepper, to taste

### FOR THE APPLE ONION RELISH

1 tbsp / 15 mL neutral-flavoured cooking oil (such as canola), for frying

1 medium onion, cut into ½-inch / 1-cm dice

1 tsp / 5 mL black mustard seeds

3 apples, peeled, cored, and cut into ½-inch / 1-cm dice (choose sweet varieties such as Braeburn, Jonagold, small Honeycrisp, Ambrosia, etc.)

2 tsp / 5 mL apple cider vinegar

1 tsp / 5 mL Dijon mustard

½ tsp / 2.5 mL salt

### FOR SERVING

½ cup / 125 mL butter, melted

8 sprigs rosemary, tied into bundles of 2 or 4 (depends on servings)

1  About 30 minutes before you want to serve this meal, take the steak out of the fridge to bring it to room temperature.

2  Combine the celeriac and cream in a small saucepan. Bring the mixture to a boil over medium heat. Reduce the heat to a simmer, cover, and cook for about 25 minutes, or until the celeriac is tender all the way through. Remove the pan from the heat. Transfer the mixture to a blender, add the butter, and purée until smooth. Season with salt. Set aside. >>

3   In a skillet, heat the oil over medium-high heat until
    it shimmers. Add the onions and black mustard
    seeds, and cook, stirring occasionally, until the
    onions are deep golden, about 10 minutes. Stir in
    the apples, cider vinegar, and mustard, and cook for
    another 5 to 10 minutes, until the apples are soft but
    retain their shape. Season with salt.

4   Preheat a grill to high (550°F / 285°C).

5   Brush the grill with oil. Season the steaks with salt
    and pepper. Grill the steaks for about 2 minutes per
    side. Reduce the heat to medium (375°F / 190°C)
    and cook for another 5 minutes or until the internal
    temperature reaches 140°F / 60°C. Transfer the
    steaks to a plate, tent with foil, and let rest for about
    5 minutes.

6   Spoon some celeriac cream onto each plate (or on a
    cutting board) and top with a steak. Give each guest
    a ramekin of apple onion relish and a ramekin of
    melted butter with a sprig of rosemary alongside so
    everyone can brush their steaks with butter at the
    table.

# RUBBED SAGE LEG OF VENISON WITH ROOT VEGETABLE SALAD, LENTILS, AND FOREST MUSHROOM BUNDLES

MAKES 4 TO 6 SERVINGS

Venison is deer meat, and the leg is very lean, so you don't want to cook it past medium-rare. Some people believe venison tastes too "gamey" — that's because its flavour depends on what the animal has been eating and how hard or easy its life has been that season. Here I pair it with the strong flavours of cinnamon, nutmeg, and rubbed sage. In fact, this seasoning mix is incredible with all types of game meat. It's also delicious when paired with another forest flavour: mushrooms. Be sure to use rubbed sage (see Tip on page 55) as it has a superior flavour to ground dried sage, which can quickly get musty and stale in the cupboard.

## FOR THE JUNIPER DRESSING

¼ cup / 60 mL mayonnaise

½ tsp / 2.5 mL porcini powder

½ tsp / 2.5 mL dried juniper berries (about 8), crushed to a fine powder (see Tip on page 189)

2 tbsp / 30 mL water

1 tbsp / 15 mL good-quality organic honey (see page 134)

¼ tsp / 1 mL salt

## FOR THE SHAVED ROOT VEGETABLE SALAD

1 medium red beet, peeled

1 medium candy cane beet, peeled

1 parsnip, peeled

2 tbsp / 30 mL canola oil

Fleur de sel, to taste

## FOR THE VENISON RUB AND VENISON

2 lbs / 900 g venison leg meat, deboned

6 tbsp / 90 mL rubbed sage

2 tbsp / 30 mL salt

1 tbsp / 15 mL freshly ground black pepper

1 tbsp / 15 mL granulated garlic

1 tsp / 5 mL ground cinnamon

1 tsp / 5 mL ground nutmeg

2 tbsp / 30 mL canola oil

½ cup / 125 mL mossberries or saskatoon berries

## FOR THE LENTILS

2 cups / 500 mL red, green, or brown lentils

1 tbsp / 15 mL Minced Garlic and Shallots in Oil (recipe page 282)

3 tbsp / 45 mL butter

½ cup / 125 mL Pheasant Broth (recipe page 276), Bison Bone Broth (recipe page 280), or good-quality chicken broth

Salt and freshly ground black pepper, to taste

## FOR THE MUSHROOM BUNDLES

4 to 6 cups / 1 to 1.5 L mixed mushrooms (shiitake, king, beech)

¼ cup / 60 mL Minced Garlic and Shallots in Oil (recipe page 282)

¼ cup / 60 mL butter

Salt and freshly ground black pepper, to taste

1   *Make the dressing:* Whisk together the mayonnaise, porcini powder, juniper powder, water, honey, and salt in a bowl until emulsified.

2   *Make the salad:* Using the thinnest setting on your mandoline slicer, or your precision knife skills, cut the beets and the parsnip into very thin slices, about ⅛ inch / 3 mm.

3   Heat the oil in a skillet over medium-high heat until it shimmers. One at a time, cook the sliced vegetables for 8 to 10 minutes, just until softened: Start with the parsnips and then transfer to a small bowl and set aside. Then cook the beets and set aside in a separate bowl. Let cool to room temperature. Divide the dressing evenly between the parsnips and the beets, and toss to coat. Season each with a pinch of fleur de sel. Set aside.

4   Take the venison out of the fridge about 30 minutes before cooking to bring it to room temperature.

5   *Cook the lentils:* Combine the lentils, garlic shallot mix, butter, broth, salt, and pepper in a pot. Bring to a boil over high heat, then reduce the heat and simmer (see sidebar on page 189).

6   Preheat the oven to 350°F / 180°C (see Tip on page 189).

7   *Prepare the mushroom bundles:* Divide the mushrooms into 4 even portions. Place each in the middle of a 12-inch / 30-cm square of aluminum foil. To each foil package, add 1 tbsp / 15 mL garlic shallot mix and 1 tbsp / 15 mL butter. Season with salt and pepper, to taste. Tightly close up the packages. Set aside.

8   *Make the rub and cook the venison:* Combine the sage, salt, pepper, garlic, cinnamon, and nutmeg in a bowl. Using your hands, coat all sides of the venison leg with as much of the rub as you can make stick.

9   Heat a cast iron pan over high heat. Add the 2 tbsp / 30 mL of oil and swirl to coat the bottom of the pan. Sear the venison for about 2 minutes on each side, until browned. Transfer the pan to the preheated oven and cook until the internal temperature reaches 125°F / 52°C to 130°F / 54°C (medium-rare), 20 to 30 minutes. About 10 minutes before the venison is finished, place the mushroom bundles on the same pan and roast alongside the venison. Remove the pan from the oven, transfer the venison to a cutting board and cover loosely with aluminum foil, and set aside the mushroom bundles. Let rest for about 10 minutes.

10  *Assemble the dish:* To serve, cut the venison against the grain and on an angle into 1-inch / 2.5-cm slices. Arrange on a large platter or cutting board with the dressed beets and parsnips, mushroom bundles, and lentils alongside. Scatter the mossberries or saskatoon berries on the platter or board.

TIPS

Use a mortar and pestle, or a clean spice grinder, to grind juniper berries to a fine powder.

If you are using a conventional oven, you may need to either cook the venison a little longer or increase the oven temperature by 25°F / 4°C.

**RED, ORANGE, AND YELLOW LENTILS** break down the most and will be ready in 30 minutes. Brown and black lentils will be ready in 20 to 30 minutes. Beluga lentils need only about 15 minutes to cook, as they are relatively small. Green lentils, also called lentils du Puy, are large and firm and need 30 to 40 minutes cooking time. For all lentils, cook until soft throughout but intact. The cooking time will also depend on their age; older lentils will take longer to cook.

# BRAISED VENISON SHANKS WITH MOSSBERRY BLACK GARLIC GLAZE AND HERBED WHEAT BERRIES

MAKES 4 SERVINGS

Wild game is usually more flavourful but a little tougher than domesticated animals. Braising, which is cooking in a small amount of liquid in a pot with a tight-fitting lid, leaves meat melt-in-your-mouth tender. It's a classic method for cooking game shanks of any kind, or even shoulder. The sweet-and-savoury flavour of the black garlic glaze adds a lot of depth to the dish, and the wheat berries are malty and chewy. (You'll need to soak the wheat berries overnight before cooking them.)

After your meal, save the shank bones. You can use the bones as a garnish the next time you make this, stuffing them with whatever herbs or greenery you like.

### FOR THE WHEAT BERRIES

1 cup / 250 mL wheat berries

3 cups / 750 mL water

6 to 8 sprigs fresh thyme

2 sprigs fresh rosemary

1 shallot, sliced

½ tsp / 2.5 mL salt

### FOR THE BRAISED VENISON SHANKS

3 cups / 750 mL all-purpose flour

3 tsp / 15 mL salt

1 tsp / 5 mL freshly ground black pepper

4 x 1-lb / 450-g red deer shanks, cross cut (bone in)

3 tbsp / 45 mL olive oil

1 tbsp / 15 mL butter

4 to 6 cups / 1 to 1.5 L Bison Bone Broth (recipe page 276)

1 carrot, roughly chopped

1 rib celery, roughly chopped

1 white onion, roughly chopped

1 bulb garlic, separated into cloves and peeled

2 tbsp / 30 mL whole black peppercorns

2 bay leaves (fresh or dried)

8 wild or green onions, for garnish

1 tbsp / 15 mL minced garlic

1 medium zucchini, diced

### FOR MOSSBERRY BLACK GARLIC GLAZE

½ cup / 125 mL mossberries (see sidebar on page 193)

⅓ cup / 80 mL black garlic cloves (about 30; see page 164)

5 tbsp / 75 mL canola oil, divided

¼ cup / 60 mL good-quality organic honey (see page 134)

Juice of ½ lemon

1   *Soak the wheat berries*: Place the wheat berries in a bowl or saucepan and cover by at least 1 inch / 2.5 cm of cold water. Soak overnight.

2   *Prepare the braised shanks:* Combine the flour, 3 tsp / 15 mL of the salt, and the black pepper in a shallow dish. Pat the deer shanks dry with paper towel and dredge them in the seasoned flour to coat completely. Tap off any excess flour.

3   In a deep, heavy skillet, Dutch oven, or pot with a tight-fitting lid, heat the olive oil and butter over medium-high heat. Sear the shanks, browning nicely on all sides, for about 2 minutes total. Transfer the shanks to a plate and set aside; reserve pan.

4   Pour the bison bone broth into the reserved pan and cook, scraping up the browned bits from the bottom of the pan, for about 5 minutes. Stir in the chopped carrot, celery, white onion, garlic, peppercorns, and bay leaves. Return the browned shanks to the pan, bone sticking up and ensuring that the liquid reaches halfway or three-quarters up the shank. Reduce the heat to medium-low and bring to a simmer. Cover and cook for 1½ hours, or until the meat is very tender and pulls away from the bone. Check the liquid level every 20 or 30 minutes, adding a bit more broth or even water, if necessary, to ensure the shanks stay covered in the broth.

5   *Cook the wheat berries:* Meanwhile, drain the wheat berries, discarding the soaking liquid. Transfer them to a pot and add 3 cups / 750 mL of cold water and the thyme, rosemary, shallot, and salt. Bring to a gentle boil over medium heat. Cover partially with a lid and cook until the wheat berries start to split their skins, about 1 hour (they should be tender but chewy). Drain, and discard the herbs and shallot pieces. Set aside.

6   *Make the glaze and finish the shanks:* Combine the mossberries, black garlic, 2 tbsp / 30 mL canola oil, honey, and lemon juice in a blender or food processor and purée until smooth. Set aside.

7   Preheat a grill to medium-high (350°F / 180°C) or preheat your oven's broiler to high.

8   Brush the wild onions with 1 tbsp / 15 mL canola oil. Grill or broil until bright green and wilted with nice char marks, 30 seconds to 1 minutes. Set aside.

9   Remove the shanks from the braising liquid and brush with the mossberry black garlic sauce. Grill, or place on a pan and broil, for 2 to 3 minutes per side, just until the sauce caramelizes (watch carefully so it doesn't burn). Discard the braising liquid.

10  *Sauté the zucchini and warm the wheat berries:* Heat 2 tbsp / 30 mL canola oil in a skillet over medium-high heat until it shimmers. Add the minced garlic and cook for about 2 minutes, just until fragrant. Add the zucchini and cook until just tender, about 5 minutes. Add the prepared wheat berries and cook, stirring occasionally, for about 5 minutes, until the wheat berries are warmed through. Cover to keep warm.

11  *Assemble the dish:* Arrange 1 shank per serving plate, along with even amounts of the wheat berries and grilled wild onions.

**MOSSBERRIES** (*Empetrum nigrum*, also called crowberries) are not super sweet but have a pleasant tannic dryness and woodsy flavour. They can be found in the Canadian north and Alaska on small evergreen shrubs that grow close to the ground. The berries sweeten after the first frost but also a bit when cooked. Their saskatoon berry–like flavour goes well with deer (aka venison) or any other game meat such as elk, moose, caribou/reindeer, bison, or antelope. If you can't find mossberries, substitute juniper berries, saskatoon berries, or red currants, which are classic flavour companions to game. Depending on the sweetness of the berries you choose for this recipe, you may want to adjust the amount of honey you use.

# CHOCOLATE BEET CAKE WITH SASKATOON BERRIES

MAKES 1 LOAF | SPECIAL EQUIPMENT: RUBBER OR LATEX GLOVES (OPTIONAL)

In June and July, when there are too many zucchinis coming out of the garden, we shred them and make chocolate zucchini cake. In the winter, I make a different version with shredded beets. The earthiness of the beets goes great with dark chocolate. This cake is delicious topped with saskatoon berries pulled from the freezer and coated with sugar. As the berries thaw in the sugar, you get a nice syrupy fruit topping. (This recipe is adapted from Nigel Slater's moist chocolate beet cake.)

1   Arrange an oven rack in the centre position. Preheat the oven to 350°F / 180°C (see Tip on page 195). Grease a 9¼- by 5¼-inch / 23.5- by 13-cm loaf pan. Set aside.

2   Place the beets in a saucepan with the salt and cover with cold water. Bring to a boil, reduce the heat, and simmer for 30 minutes or until you can easily slide a sharp knife into the centre of the beets. Drain and rinse under cold running water until cool enough to handle. Using your hands, rub off the beet skins (you may want to wear rubber or latex gloves to avoid staining your hands). Using the large holes of a box grater, grate the beets (you should end up with about 1½ cups / 375 mL). Set aside.

3   Sift together the flour, cocoa, baking powder, and salt in a bowl. Set aside.

4   Break or roughly chop the chocolate into about a dozen pieces. Transfer to a microwave-safe bowl (large enough to later accommodate the egg yolks and beets) and heat in a microwave at 50% power for 4 minutes. Keep an eye on it and take it out just as the chocolate melts. Alternatively, fill a pot with a few inches of water and set a stainless steel bowl on top to create a water bath (the bowl shouldn't touch the water). Bring the water to a boil and then add the chopped chocolate to the bowl. Heat, stirring until the chocolate has completely melted.

2 to 3 medium red beets (about 8 oz / 225 g total), unpeeled and tops trimmed

½ tsp / 2.5 mL salt

1 cup / 250 mL all-purpose flour

3 tbsp / 45 mL unsweetened cocoa powder

1¼ tsp / 6 mL baking powder

¼ tsp / 1 mL sea salt

7 oz / 200 g dark (70%) chocolate, chopped

¼ cup / 60 mL hot water

¾ cup / 175 mL + 2 tbsp / 30 mL unsalted butter (7 oz / 200g), at room temperature

5 large eggs, at room temperature, separated

1¼ cups / 310 mL granulated sugar, divided

2 cups / 500 mL saskatoon berries

5   Add the hot water to the melted chocolate and stir to combine. Cut the butter into pieces and stir into the chocolate mixture until completely incorporated. Let cool for 5 minutes.

6   Whisk the egg yolks in a bowl until frothy. Stir them into the cooled chocolate mixture. Fold in the shredded beets until well combined. Set aside.

7   Either by hand or using a stand mixer fitted with the whisk attachment, beat the egg whites to stiff peaks. Reduce the speed to low and then slowly pour in 1 cup / 250 mL of the sugar. Mix until well combined.

8   Using a spatula, fold the chocolate-beet mixture into the egg whites just until combined. Fold in the flour mixture just until combined.

9   Scrape the batter into the prepared loaf pan. Bake in the preheated oven for 1 hour, or until a toothpick inserted into the middle of the loaf slides out cleanly.

10  Meanwhile, remove the saskatoon berries from the freezer and put them in a shallow dish. Sprinkle with the remaining ¼ cup / 60 mL sugar and set aside.

11  When the cake is ready, remove the pan from the oven. Let the cake cool completely in the pan. Once cool, carefully invert the cake onto a serving plate. Cut into thick slices and serve with a generous heap of the syrupy saskatoon berries.

---

**TIP**

If you are using a conventional oven, you may need to either bake the cake a little longer or increase the oven temperature by 25°F / 4°C.

# WILD GINGER ROSEHIP TEA WITH HONEY

MAKES 2 CUPS (500 ML)

Fresh or dried Canadian wild ginger (*Asarum canadense*) or Western wild ginger (*Asarum caudatum*) has a mild peppery flavour. It grows in dense clumps on the forest floor. Use the roots only. It has been used for generations as a spice, but traditionally it is diluted and used as a tea and in medicinal applications. Some sources warn that wild ginger contains toxic compounds that can cause serious kidney issues in very large doses, but steeping it in water seems to be a safe way to consume it. Enjoy this tea as a special treat only.

The ginger in this tea has a nice warming effect and the rosehip provides a slight acidity and is also a good source of vitamin C.

1    Using a mortar and pestle, muddle the ginger stems and roots with the rosehips until the stems and roots are bruised and the rosehips are crushed (or at least cracked open).

2    In a small pot, bring the water to a boil. Reduce the heat and add the honey, ginger, and rosehips. Simmer for 8 to 10 minutes. Taste and add more honey, if needed. Serve hot.

5 wild ginger stems and roots

16 dried rosehip berries

2 cups / 500 mL water

1 tbsp / 15 mL good-quality organic honey (see page 134)

**THE PROVINCIAL FLOWER** of my home province, Alberta, is the wild rose (*Rosa acicularis*), so it's easy to harvest as many rosehips as we want in the woods and river valley in Edmonton. In the fall, fresh rosehips are quite tannic. It's best to wait until winter, when the leaves of the wild rose are gone and the blood-red rosehips are all that are left on the low, thorny bushes. Rosehips are sweeter and less tannic after they have had a good freeze anyway.

# CHEF RYAN O'FLYNN

**A FIRST-GENERATION** white guy from Edmonton with Irish-Welsh blood may seem like an unlikely champion of the Indigenous culinary perspective, but Ryan is such a visionary, and along with his insane cooking talent and discipline, I am always inspired by what he has to say and the food he cooks.

Ryan and I went to the same culinary school, but for Ryan, the expectations were huge: His dad, Maurice O'Flynn, was a big deal in Canada's culinary community. Ryan wisely struck out on his own and left for Europe to build his resumé and skills. At the age of 24, he became head chef at Wales' top restaurant at the time, Le Gallois. He then worked at Pétrus, a Gordon Ramsay Michelin-starred restaurant in Knightsbridge, London. At the age of 29, he finished his European decade as executive chef across the street from Buckingham Palace at the Milestone Hotel, a five-star boutique hotel in Kensington that was voted best hotel in the world by Condé Nast.

When he returned to Canada, Ryan came back to Edmonton. I like that. With his passion and experience, he wanted to show that food in Edmonton could be just as good as anywhere else. In 2015, Ryan competed in Gold Medal Plates and won. That took him to the Canadian Culinary Championships, a big deal of a professional culinary competition that includes the top chefs from across Canada who have also won in their respective cities. He won that, too.

With his extensive experience at Europe's top restaurants, he recognized the untapped value of wild Canadian ingredients, and he acknowledged Indigenous culinary traditions. He spent time with the Dene, whose territory is up in the northern boreal and Canadian Arctic regions. He is now creating informed and exciting food, helping us open our eyes to the potential of what Canadian food can be.

It means a lot to me that he's agreed to be a part of my book.

# REDISCOVERING INDIGENOUS TERROIR

## BY CHEF RYAN O'FLYNN

**I JUST WANT PEOPLE** to eat properly—according to their terroir.

In Europe, people travel to find a chef who is cooking from her or his own heart, who has her or his own identity, who's not copying things off Instagram, and who's making food that is original. People find out about that, and they line up. Although we have some fantastic, legit, and creative restaurants in Alberta, what we tend to do is copy and paste. It happens far too often. It's temporary crap. It's garbage. We watch for a trend coming from California or New York, wait a year, dumb it down, and do it half as well.

If I'm going to say anything, it's that the only way we're ever going to move our country's food forward is to take our identity—which already exists, by the way, and has been here much longer than any of us Westerners—and serve it up in a world-class restaurant. We have this amazing First Nations diversity. It rivals anything in Europe. How many different Indigenous cultures are there from Victoria, British Columbia, to St. John's, Newfoundland? Each and every one has its own stories, its own myths, and all the creative arts that come with a culture. It's our strength, and we turn a blind eye to it. Instead, we're trying to be American or European, and we do a very shitty job at it. And what's happened is that there's a lot of good out there but fuck-all that is amazing and real.

Canadian chefs need to look toward First Nations' smoking and preserving cooking methods and way of looking at the world, as well as the arts of the Haida Gwaii, the Dene, the Dogrib, and the Mohawk. We need to ask what they have to offer. Let's go learn from them. Indigenous art should be at the forefront of most things Canadian.

I got to spend time with the Dene in northern Canada a few years back. I learned how to make bannock with fish roe, and how to smoke meats with rotten birch stumps (you have to make sure you don't get them mixed up with rotten poplar stumps...not the same result), and how to build tripods over the fire. Just by being there, listening and learning, I was able to create one of the most amazing bison dishes that I've ever done: rib of wood bison, smoked in a rotten birch stump and basted in wild northern birch syrup with smoked roots, black barley, and a carrot purée that resembled the wildfires of the northwest that give us our morel mushrooms around Mother's Day the following season. Is it First Nations cuisine? No. Does it have elements of it? Totally. Being around the Dene and learning from the Elders inspired me to do food that's smart, elegant, thoughtful, and Canadian.

Until we showcase the rich cultures and traditions that surround us, we will remain a place where people come to see our mountains while eating really bad deep-fried pastry and plastic chocolate.

The key will be to keep our cuisine authentic. We're not going after any Michelin stars or Rosettes. It's smoked bison. It's smoked elk. It's taking that winter casserole but adding some Northwest Territories morels or Saskatchewan chanterelles to those northern beans. Or incorporating botanicals from the forest. It's smoking and preserving. It's expressing the pure beauty of places like Tofino, Yellowknife, and Fort Providence alike. All of that energy can be focussed in any place, from a three-star Michelin restaurant to a corner brasserie or a truck stop.

It's Métis somehow—what happens when Indigenous and non-Indigenous people come together and create something organically and in an unforced way, but through food. We've got to stop looking at the United States and Europe for inspiration, and instead look within ourselves. Only then will people start looking to us.

The way I see it is that we need to be more "Fuck you! Here we are. Come and get us." Sure, there's risk to this sort of approach. But if you can grasp the concept of Indigenous terroir and turn it into something that enough people understand, it will be timeless, not trendy. We just need to figure out what "it" is.

Maybe Shane's the guy to help us? He's about emotions and dreams and thoughts. I love reading his social media posts, because he's definitely on a journey. He doesn't give a shit. He's still searching and it's cool to see. He has nothing to copy and paste from. He goes first.

^>⁰

*pipon*

# WINTER

# WINTER

# GALETTE WITH ROASTED GARLIC TWO WAYS

MAKES 1 GALETTE

We have a few treasured family recipes that are typically reserved for when we can get together during holidays: my mom's pickled beets and her pistachio pudding, and my dad's galette. My dad is Métis, and he inherited this recipe from his family. "Galette" is Michif (the Métis language) for *bannock* (see page 287 for a brief discussion of the other words used for this popular First Nations quickrise bread). Dad's galette is a dense crumb. I like to eat this bread with soft, roasted garlic or garlic purée.

1 *Roast the garlic:* Preheat the oven to 225°F / 110°C (see Tip on page 210). Set aside a muffin pan with at least a 6-cup capacity. Using a sharp knife, slice the tops off the garlic bulbs so just the tips of the cloves are exposed. Brush the cut tops with a generous amount of olive oil and place each bulb in a well of the muffin cup. Bake for 1 to 1½ hours, or until the top of the bulbs are golden and the garlic is very soft. Remove the pan from the oven. Drizzle each clove with a bit of olive oil and sprinkle with a pinch of fleur de sel. Tent with aluminum foil to keep warm.

2 *Make the garlic purée:* Preheat the oven to 325°F / 170°C (see Tip on page 210). Combine the garlic cloves, oil, and a pinch of salt and pepper in a bowl and toss until the garlic is well coated. Transfer to a large square of aluminum foil and seal the packet tightly. Roast in the preheated oven for about 30 minutes, or until the garlic is tender and golden. Using a small blender or immersion blender, purée until smooth (add a little water if it's too thick; it should be the consistency of hummus).

3 *Make the galette:* Decrease the oven temperature to 300°F / 150°C (see Tip on page 210). Line a baking sheet with parchment paper. >>

## FOR THE ROASTED GARLIC

4 to 6 garlic bulbs (see Tip on page 210)

Olive oil, for roasting and for drizzling

Fleur de sel

## FOR THE GARLIC PURÉE

1 cup / 250 mL cloves garlic, peeled

2 tbsp / 30 mL olive oil

Salt and freshly ground black pepper, to taste

## FOR THE GALETTE

6 cups / 1.5 L all-purpose flour

6 tbsp / 90 mL baking powder

2 tbsp + 1½ tsp / 37.5 mL salt

¾ cup / 175 mL canola oil

2 cups / 500 mL whole milk, or more if needed

Fleur de sel, for finishing the dough

## FOR THE EGG WASH

1 egg

¼ cup / 60 mL milk

4  In the bowl of a stand mixer fitted with the dough hook attachment, combine the flour, baking powder, salt, and oil. Add the milk and mix just until a shaggy dough has formed (if needed, add more milk, a tablespoon at a time, until you reach the right consistency). Turn out onto a lightly floured work surface and knead a few times to bring everything together—the dough should still be shaggy.

5  Using your hands, shape the dough into a log 15 inches / 38 cm long, 6 inches / 15 cm wide, and 1 inch / 2.5 cm tall. Place on the prepared baking sheet. Flatten the top, and then using your fingers, press deep divots into the dough in rows of 4.

6  *Egg wash the dough:* Whisk together the egg and milk in a small bowl. Brush over the prepared dough. Sprinkle with fleur de sel. Bake in the preheated oven for 40 minutes, until the top just begins to turn golden brown. Remove from the oven and let cool on the pan for about 10 minutes.

7  Slice the galette into 1-inch- / 2.5-cm-thick slices and serve warm with the roasted garlic and/or purée.

---

**TIPS**

To enjoy the roasted garlic, squeeze the soft, buttery, golden garlic out of the top of each clove and spread it on the sliced bread.

---

If you are using a conventional oven, you may need to either bake the items a little longer or increase the oven temperature by 25°F / 4°C.

# ON TATTOOS

**I HAVE A LOT OF TATTOOS** and they are closely tied to my self-identity. They're meaningful to me because they show my progression as a young cook in my 20s to where I am now. In fact, if you visit my restaurant you'll see photographs of my tattoos on the walls. My journey is documented right on my skin.

### TRIBAL

I got my first tattoo when I was 20. I have to laugh at myself for this one, because it's an old "tribal" tattoo, from back when tribal was cool. I remember thinking that I might regret it someday, but I figured that no matter how old I got, or even if I didn't like it as much as the years went on, it was still a tribal tattoo and very "me." Luckily, I still like it to this day.

### BEAR, EAGLE, AND SUN

When I was 28, I got a traditional Haida Gwaii bear and eagle on each side of my chest. I really like the softness of the Haida Gwaii arts. The bear represents strength and long life. The eagle represents sight (it oversees a lot from high up). They are both symbolic of wisdom. I also have a Haida Gwaii sun on one of my calves, a symbol of healing and peace.

### SLEEVE

I've always liked sleeve tattoos. I know they're super trendy now, but I'd wanted one ever since I saw a Japanese chef with a sleeve tattoo poking out from beneath the cuff of his chef's coat. I loved the idea.

When I was 32, I had a very serious bout of pneumonia. To this day I have never been so sick. For two weeks I couldn't do anything other than sleep. I couldn't even talk on the phone. The fatigue was incredible. Once I recovered, I really wanted to do something that I'd been dreaming about, without thinking twice. That's when I started working on my sleeve. At the time I was addicted to Japanese food. I loved how clean both the flavours and techniques are. On my 33rd birthday, I started on my left arm, from shoulder to wrist. I finished my sleeve tattoo a year later, on my 34th birthday. I have a squid, artichoke, octopus, shrimp, chef's knife, blowfish, daylily, seashell, and dragon fruit. My sleeve tattoo is important to me because my interest in Japanese cooking — how culturally defined it is, and how proudly independent the flavours and techniques are — helped me find a path to creating my own style of Indigenous cooking.

### SKULL AND HEADDRESS

At the Calgary Farmers' Market, I saw a woman who had the most beautiful flower tattoo on the back of her hand. It was stunning. Right away, I knew my next tattoo would be on the back of my hand. I'd always wanted a headdress tattoo but knew they could sometimes come

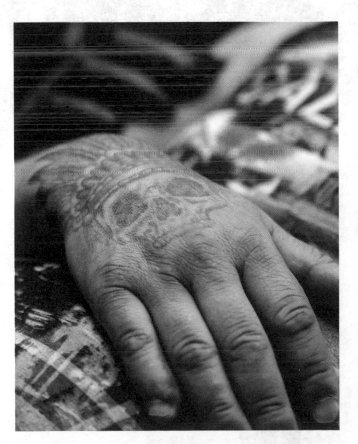

off as tacky and corny, and rarely looked good. Regardless, I took the idea to my tattoo artist, who is really into skulls, too. We created something together that I love looking at whenever I look down at my hand.

### NATIVE BRIDE

I have always wanted a beautiful female face tattooed on my skin — I'm inspired by all the beautiful Indigenous women around me! In 2018, I had a Native bride added to my right shoulder and upper arm.

### TRADITIONAL CREE HAND-POKE TATTOO

Gingolx or Kincolith is a Pacific Ocean inlet community quite far north in British Columbia, in the territory of the Nisga'a. It's one of the four main villages in the Nass Valley. I travelled there to film a documentary in 2018. During the film shoot, I met Nisga'a community members and Elders, and then I cooked with them so I could learn about their food culture. The trip had a profound impact on me because I really felt the beauty and power of the landscape there, and it made me realize that I want to experience more here rather than needing to travel to other continents or countries. It also was the place where I received my most meaningful tattoo.

Through my contacts with the documentary production company, I'd heard about a Nisga'a artist named Nakkita Trimble-Wilson who practises traditional Indigenous tattooing. Her Nisga'a name is Algaxhl Gwilks-k̲'alt'amtkw, which means "speaking through art." It was an honour to be tattooed by Nakkita. The traditional Cree design runs from my jawline to my chest, and it is my most meaningful tattoo because it ties me to my Cree ancestors.

# VISIBLY INDIGENOUS: WEARING OUR ANCESTRAL MARKS

## BY NAKKITA TRIMBLE-WILSON

**CONTACT WITH EUROPEANS** occurred roughly in the 1850s. The missionaries suppressed our Indigenous tattooing practices among other cultural traditions. A big part of the government-funded suppression of our ceremonies resulted from the Potlatch Ban of 1880. It was illegal for us to follow our way of life. Until 2014, we had not practised traditional tattooing in over 150 years.

In 2014, I met with the Council of Elders. They shared oral history of Nisga'a tattoo practices prior to contact with Europeans. The Council of Elders is comprised of some Matriarchs and Chiefs of the four main villages in the Nass Valley. The Elders are in full support of traditional tattooing for our people. I asked permission from the Elders to revive Nisga'a tattooing, and they agreed.

I practise the tattooing methods used by our ancestors, including hand poking and skin stitching. Both methods were used by our Nation as well as many other Indigenous Nations across Turtle Island. The crests or designs I tattoo are Maternal House Crest Designs that are tens of thousands of years old. These designs serve as our hereditary title over the land to which they are attached, representing our hunting, fishing, and harvesting rights. Each design belongs to a different family group or House.

When you are born, you are born into your mother's crest. Tattooing was a ceremony that was practiced within the Potlatch—as a public matter. The Elders would decide who would receive what as a tattoo. There was responsibility in receiving the design: You had to pass down the oral history attached to the design that represents the history, stories, and songs within your family.

Shane and I had our first consultations regarding what would be an appropriate cultural tattoo for him over the phone. Shane wanted a tattoo that represented his experience with the Nisga'a Nation in Gingolx. Because Shane is from a culture outside of the Nisga'a Nation, I suggested using a method both our ancestors practised: either hand poking or skin stitching.

I am not Cree, so I consulted with Cree-Métis tattoo visual artist Amy Malbeuf, who is originally from Rich Lake, Alberta. She sent me information

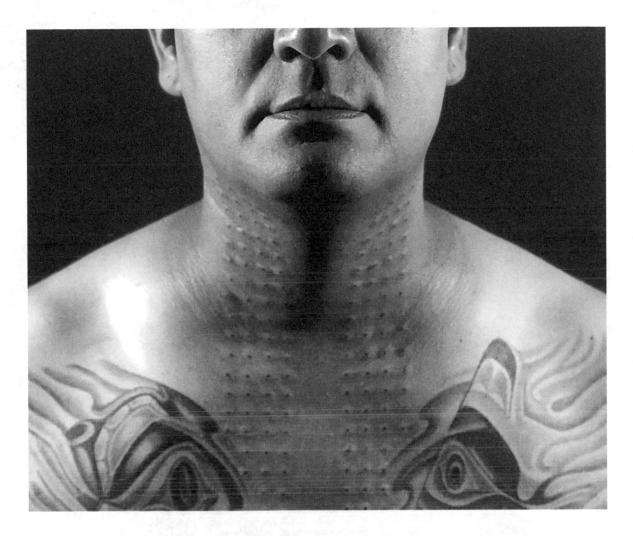

on traditional Cree tattoo designs, and Shane and I came up with the idea of replicating a traditional Cree tattoo design with lines of dots running down from his jawline to his chest, using the ancient hand-poke method.

Tattooing our ancient designs using an ancient method is a spiritual ceremony. When someone comes to me seeking this type of tattoo, research is vital. There is a responsibility in the wearer to know their history so that we accurately tattoo this history into their skin. There is also a responsibility in the tattoo artist to ensure the wearer has permission to wear the design they are seeking. I will not tattoo something someone pulled off Google. The wearer has a responsibility to consult their Elders to ensure accuracy. I will not tattoo something that does not belong to a person, as I do not want to perpetuate cultural appropriation.

The ultimate goal is to teach Indigenous artists the foundation in researching their Nation and identity so that when we train them to tattoo, they become cultural knowledge holders who accurately represent their people and keep their history alive. Indigenous groups across Turtle Island will be tattooing their own peoples' designs as this movement continues to grow.

# KOMBU SEAWEED SOUP WITH PHEASANT

MAKES 6 TO 8 SERVINGS

We've been overlooking seaweed — an abundant superfood — for far too long. It's rich in calcium, folate, iodine, magnesium, and iron, and vitamins B12, C, and K. A number of companies are now harvesting and selling seaweed so it's easier to find it in mainstream grocery stores. Be sure to look for some: It adds the perfect hit of savoury saltiness to soup and other dishes.

1   Preheat a grill to 400°F / 200°C. (Alternatively, you can cook the pheasant in a cast iron pan over medium-high heat in 1 tbsp / 15 mL canola oil.)

2   In a medium saucepan, heat the oil until it shimmers. Add the celery, shallot, minced garlic, onion, leek, and kombu flakes and cook until the vegetables have softened, about 10 minutes. Set aside.

3   Brush the pheasant breasts with canola oil and lightly season both sides with salt and pepper. Brush the hot grill with oil. Cook the breast meat on the hot grill or in the cast iron pan for 2 to 3 minutes per side (don't worry if the pheasant is still a little pink; it will finish cooking in the soup). Transfer the cooked pheasant to a plate and let rest for at least 5 minutes. Using a sharp knife, working against the grain, cut the breast into bite-size cubes. Set aside.

4   In a large soup pot, bring the broth to a simmer. Add the vegetables and the diced meat, along with the white vinegar and duck fat (if using). Bring back to a simmer and cook for 15 to 20 minutes, until the vegetables are tender and the pheasant is fully cooked. Taste, season with salt and pepper, if necessary, and serve hot.

3 tbsp / 45 mL canola oil

2 ribs celery, cut into medium dice

1 large shallot, minced

¼ cup / 60 mL minced garlic

1 medium white onion, cut into small dice

1 leek, white parts only, cut into small dice

1 oz / 28 g dried large-flake kombu seaweed, broken up into pieces

2 pheasant, chicken, or duck breasts, skin on, or 1 goose breast

Salt and freshly ground black pepper, to taste

6 cups / 1.5 L Pheasant Broth (recipe page 280) or good-quality chicken broth

½ cup / 125 mL white vinegar

3 tbsp / 45 mL duck fat (optional)

# TURKEY NECK SOUP

MAKES 3 TO 6 SERVINGS | SPECIAL EQUIPMENT: PRESSURE COOKER (OPTIONAL)

This is a Chartrand family favourite, especially around Christmas, and we like to get into it with our hands: We chew around the cartilage on the neck, and then we just drink the broth. No spoons! But obviously eat this however you feel most comfortable.

1   Combine the turkey necks, broth, carrots, onion, and garlic in a pressure cooker. Seal the lid and cook for 25 minutes (follow the manufacturer's instructions). Release the steam and open the pressure cooker when safe. If you don't have a pressure cooker, combine the same ingredients in a soup pot and simmer over medium-low heat for about 2 hours, until the meat comes away from the neck and the vegetables are soft.

2   Season the soup with salt and pepper. Garnish with the sliced green onions and pea shoots. Serve in large soup bowls — with or without a spoon.

6 turkey necks

8 cups / 2 L Pheasant Broth (recipe page 280) or good-quality chicken broth

2 large carrots, roughly chopped

1 large white onion, roughly chopped

5 to 6 cloves garlic, peeled

Salt and freshly ground black pepper, to taste

4 green onions, finely sliced at an angle

½ cup / 125 mL pea shoots

# CLAMS COOKED IN WINTER ALE

MAKES 4 SERVINGS

Clams are so very abundant and a great sustainable seafood choice. As you would for mussels, make sure they are healthy and alive before they go into the pot: Store them in the refrigerator under a moist cloth and rinse them under cold running water just before you plan on cooking them. If a clam shell is open, give it a good rap or two. If it doesn't close up tight, discard it.

Choose whatever variety of clam is readily available to you for this recipe. Just adjust the cooking time as needed: Hard-shell clams will take longer to steam than their soft-shell cousins.

1   Set a large pot or Dutch oven over high heat. Add the oil and the red onions, red peppers, and diced jalapeño. Sauté for about 5 minutes, stirring constantly, until the onions have softened and the peppers have brightened.

2   Add the clams and ale. Cover with the lid and let the clams cook until they open wide (timing will depend on how large the clams are). Add 1 tbsp / 15 mL butter and season with salt and pepper, to taste.

3   Divide the cooked clams evenly into 4 serving bowls and garnish with the pea shoots. Serve steaming hot.

2 tbsp / 30 mL canola oil

½ red onion, thinly sliced

1 red bell pepper, seeded, cored, and thinly sliced

½ jalapeño pepper, seeded and finely diced

2 lbs / 900 g clams, scrubbed

250 mL / 1 cup winter ale

1 tbsp / 15 mL butter

1 tsp / 5 mL salt, or to taste

½ tsp / 2.5 mL freshly ground black pepper, or to taste

Pea shoots, for garnish

# SMOKED OYSTERS

MAKES 1 DOZEN OYSTERS | SPECIAL EQUIPMENT: SMOKER; YOUR CHOICE OF WOOD CHIPS

Smoking is a traditional method of cooking, not just in Indigenous cultures but almost everywhere. It's usually a long, slow process, but with oysters, it takes less than an hour.

You'll want to dedicate an old pan, skillet, or wire rack to smoking, as it will be quite something to clean after you are done. Best to just wipe it down and keep it for the next smoker adventure.

1   Start your smoker and get the temperature to a consistent 225°F / 110°C. Place the whole, unshucked oysters in a pan or on a wire rack that fits in the smoker. Close the lid and smoke the oysters for 45 minutes to an hour, depending on their size.

2   Shuck the oysters, removing the top shell (see page 36 for how to shuck oysters). Arrange the oysters on the half shell on a platter so that they are stable, sprinkle with oil and Worcestershire sauce, and finish with a pinch of fleur de sel. Serve immediately.

12 fresh oysters of your choice (oysters with a deeper cup are ideal for this recipe)

3½ tbsp / 47.5 mL cold-pressed canola oil, or olive oil, for serving

2 tbsp / 30 mL Worcestershire sauce, for serving

Fleur de sel

# GRILLED OCTOPUS SALAD

MAKES 4 SERVINGS | SPECIAL EQUIPMENT: PRESSURE COOKER

I've always had a massive infatuation with octopuses. I've got one in my sleeve tattoo. I love how they swim, how they fit through the tiniest of spaces, how they change colour. To be honest, I mostly just love how they taste, sashimi to grilled. This recipe is a version of poached and grilled octopus. I love the delicate texture of the meat, and that slight caramelized sear and smoke you get from the grill. It's perfect accompanied by a winter salad with maple vinaigrette.

When improperly cooked, octopus will be rubbery and tough. When done properly, the meat is delicate and sweetly delicious. To avoid having to soften octopus meat in a long, long poach, you can use a pressure cooker, which shortens cooking time considerably, as does choosing baby octopus. Octopus from Canada's West Coast and Alaska are Ocean Wise choices (seafood.ocean. org), but you can have a conversation about that with your local fishmonger.

### FOR THE OCTOPUS

4 or 5 baby octopuses

8 cups / 2 L Pheasant Broth (recipe page 280), Bison Bone Broth (recipe page 276), or good-quality chicken broth

6 tbsp Minced Garlic and Shallots in Oil (recipe page 282)

¼ cup / 60 mL pure maple syrup

Coarse kosher salt and freshly ground black pepper, to taste

### FOR THE SALAD

¼ cup / 60 mL lemon oil (see Tip on page 228)

2 tbsp / 30 mL bee pollen (see page 94)

1 rib celery, sliced on the bias as thinly as possible (about ½ to ¾ inch / 1 to 2 cm)

3 green onions, sliced on the bias as thinly as possible (about ½ to ¾ inch / 1 to 2 cm)

2 sprigs fresh dill, roughly chopped

¾ cup / 175 mL pea shoots

1  *Cook the octopuses:* Preheat a grill to medium (375°F / 190°C).

2  Place the octopuses, pheasant broth, and garlic shallot mix in a pressure cooker. Seal and cook for 25 minutes (follow the manufacturer's instructions). Release the steam safely, transfer the octopuses to a colander, and rinse under cold running water. Let drain.

3  *Make the salad:* Whisk together the lemon oil and bee pollen in a large bowl. Add the celery, green onions, dill, and pea shoots. Toss to coat well. >>

4   *Grill the octopuses:* Place the octopuses in a large bowl and toss with the maple syrup. Place each octopus on the hot grill, head-side up, and cook for about 2 minutes, just until the syrup caramelizes. Transfer to a tray and season with salt and pepper.

5   To serve, arrange the salad on a serving platter or shallow dish. Arrange grilled octopuses on top. Serve warm.

A totem pole in Carcross, Yukon Territory, taken on a trip to the Northwest.

**TIP**

You can buy lemon oil at an Italian grocery store, but it's also easy to make yourself (see page 49).

# BLACKENED COD WITH CELERIAC PURÉE AND CRISPY POTATO CHIPS

MAKES 4 SERVINGS

Cod has been such an important food to the East Coast of Canada for thousands of years, but in just my lifetime, the disastrous effects of over-fishing Atlantic cod have come to bear. Most Pacific cod from the West Coast is now sustainably caught using methods that don't scrape up the ocean floor, and sustainable fishing practices for cod now create minimal bycatch. It's important to be very wary and specific when buying this fish.

## FOR THE SHAVED POTATO CHIPS

2 large russet potatoes

6 cups (1.5 L) cold water

½ cup / 125 mL white vinegar

Neutral-flavoured cooking oil (such as canola), for frying

Fleur de sel

## FOR THE CELERIAC PURÉE

1 cup / 250 mL half-and-half (10%) cream

2 cups / 500 mL peeled, diced celeriac root, about ½ lb / 225 g

¼ cup / 60 mL butter

Salt, to taste

## FOR THE BLACKENING SEASONING

3 tbsp / 45 mL ground cayenne pepper

3 tbsp / 45 mL coarse kosher salt

2 tbsp / 30 mL raw sesame seeds, toasted

1 tbsp / 15 mL ground cumin

1 tbsp / 15 mL onion powder

1½ tbsp / 17.5 mL freshly ground black pepper

1 tbsp / 15 mL crushed nori (see Tip)

1 tbsp / 15 mL Togarashi seasoning

## FOR THE COD

4 x 1-lb / 450-g cod fillets, skinned

2 tbsp / 30 mL canola oil, or more if needed

4 carrot top greens, or any other feathery green herb like chervil, dill fronds, or flat-leaf parsley, for garnish

---

**TIP**

For the crushed nori, simply crush a small sheet of nori in a mortar and pestle or your fingers until the size of fleur de sel flakes.

1   *Prepare the shaved potatoes*: Peel the potatoes. Using a mandoline on the thinnest setting, or your precision knife skills, cut the potatoes into ⅛-inch- / 3-mm-thick slices. Place the potato slices in a colander and rinse under cold running water for a few minutes until the water runs clear. Fill a large bowl with about 6 cups / 1.5 L cold water and ½ cup / 125 mL white vinegar. Put the potato slices in the vinegar water and set aside for about 20 minutes.

2   Meanwhile, fill a heavy-bottomed pot with about 4 inches / 10 cm of canola oil and heat to 300°F / 150°C.

3   Drain the potatoes and pat dry with a clean cloth or paper towel. Working in batches so as not to crowd the pan, deep-fry the potatoes until golden, about 5 minutes per batch, using a wire-mesh scoop or slotted spoon to gently move the potato slices around in the oil as they fry. Transfer to paper towel and season with fleur de sel. (These can be made hours ahead and stored, uncovered, at room temperature until ready to serve.)

4   *Make the celeriac purée:* In a heavy pot, combine the cream, celeriac, and butter. Bring to a low simmer (just until it's steaming but not boiling) and cook until the celeriac cubes are soft, about 20 minutes. Remove the pan from the heat and let cool. Once cooled, transfer to a blender and purée until smooth. Season with salt.

5   *Make the blackening seasoning:* Combine the cayenne pepper, salt, sesame seeds, cumin, onion powder, black pepper, crushed nori, and Togarashi in a shallow dish. Mix well. Lay the cod fillets in the seasoning and turn to coat all sides evenly.

6   *Cook the cod:* Heat a couple of tablespoons of canola oil in a nonstick or cast iron skillet over medium-high heat until it shimmers. Sear the fish for about 3 minutes per side, or until the flesh turns opaque and flakes easily with a fork.

7   *Assemble the dish:* Place a generous dollop of celeriac purée on each of 4 serving plates. Lay a piece of cod at an angle on part of the celeriac. Grab a handful of fried potato chips and arrange them beside the cod on the celeriac. Garnish with a sprig of your favourite feathery herb — I like to use carrot top fronds as a garnish.

# GRILLED HERRING WITH FENNEL CREAM AND FENNEL SLAW

MAKES 4 SERVINGS

Even though we have a herring fishery here in Canada, it's definitely an underutilized fish. Herring are a forage fish, meaning that they eat at the base of the food chain and are the dinner of many of the other fish that we eat. There are two herring seasons, November and January, on both our West and East coasts. The fish are smaller in November than in January, and in general Pacific herring are smaller than Atlantic herring. Herring can be an abundant food source when caught sustainably, and there are plenty of options right here on Canada's West Coast, East Coast, and in the St. Lawrence gulf. Often you have to make special requests for herring from your fishmonger, but they are a delicious, mild-flavoured fish when grilled or seared in a hot cast iron pan.

### FOR THE FENNEL CREAM

1 fennel bulb, roughly chopped or sliced on a mandoline

½ white onion, chopped

2 tbsp / 30 mL unsalted butter

¼ cup / 60 mL dry white wine

½ cup / 125 mL fennel fronds, chopped

2 cups / 500 mL whipping (35%) cream

Salt and freshly ground black pepper, to taste

### FOR THE FENNEL SLAW

1 fennel bulb

2 cups / 500 mL freshly squeezed orange juice (about 8 oranges)

1 tbsp / 15 mL freshly squeezed lemon juice

¼ cup / 60 mL chopped fresh basil leaves, mint leaves, or dill fronds

Salt, to taste

### FOR THE HERRING

8 herring, gutted and scaled

1 tbsp / 15 mL olive oil, plus a bit more for the grill

Coarse kosher salt, to taste

1   *Make the fennel cream:* Combine the fennel and onion with the butter and wine in a skillet. Cook over medium heat for 15 to 20 minutes, until the vegetables are translucent and soft. Add the fronds and cream and simmer for 25 minutes, until very fragrant. Let cool for about 10 minutes, then transfer the mixture to a blender and purée until smooth. Using a fine-mesh sieve, strain into an airtight container (discard solids). Season with salt and pepper, to taste. Cover and refrigerate until ready to use.

2   *Make the slaw:* Thinly slice the fennel using a mandoline or sharp knife. Transfer to a saucepan, add the orange and lemon juice, and bring to a simmer. Cook for 15 minutes, until the fennel is soft but still retains its shape. Remove the pan from the heat and let steep for another 15 minutes. Drain and let cool. Stir in the fresh herbs and season with salt.

3   *Grill the herring:* Heat a grill to high (450°F / 230°C). If you don't have a charcoal grill, get a couple of cast iron pans very hot and add a drizzle of oil. Rub the outside and inside cavities of the herring with oil and sprinkle generously with coarse salt. Place on the preheated grill and cook for 3 to 4 minutes per side, until the skin gets very crispy, the eyes turn white and opaque, and the flesh is firm (don't flip until the skin gets nice and crisp).

4   To serve, place 2 herring on each serving plate with a generous mound of both the fennel cream and the fennel slaw alongside. When eating, it's totally okay to use your hands to peel the herring skin and dip it into the fennel cream.

# TURKEY TORTELLINI WITH CREAMED WILD RICE

MAKES 6 SERVINGS | SPECIAL EQUIPMENT: PASTA ROLLER

Thomas Keller's recipe for pasta dough (from his important 1999 cookbook, *The French Laundry*) is the first pasta recipe I ever learned and the only one I've used since then. The only alteration I've made is to use canola oil instead of olive oil — because it's from the Canadian Prairies. Of course, the turkey tortellini filling and the wild rice are my own Indigenous spins. And since tortellini is so late-1990s, I just had to go with a rich cream sauce!

### FOR THE PASTA DOUGH

8 oz / 225 g all-purpose flour (about 1¾ cups / 425 mL)

1 large egg

6 large egg yolks

1½ tsp / 7 mL canola oil

1 tbsp / 15 mL milk (2% or 3.25%)

### FOR THE TORTELLINI FILLING

2 tbsp / 30 mL canola oil

1 cup / 250 mL diced onion

6 oz / 170 g ground turkey

6 fresh sage leaves, finely minced

1 large egg

¼ cup / 60 mL whipping (35%) cream

¼ tsp / 1 mL salt, or to taste

¼ tsp / 1 mL freshly ground black pepper, or to taste

### FOR THE WILD RICE

1 ½ cups / 375 mL water

½ cup / 125 mL wild rice, rinsed and drained

½ cup / 125 mL whipping (35%) cream

Salt and freshly ground black pepper, to taste

½ cup / 125 mL freshly grated Parmesan cheese (optional), for serving

1   *Make the pasta dough:* On a clean, non-porous surface or a large wooden cutting board, shape the flour into a mound with a 6-inch / 15-cm crater in the centre. Put the egg and yolks, oil, and milk in the centre. Using your fingers, break the yolks and start to swirl the wet ingredients with your fingers, but don't let the inside of the crater break through the flour sides. As you continue to swirl, the flour will very slowly incorporate into the eggs. Be patient and keep swirling. You can start to use your other hand to shore up the sides and move some of the flour into the egg mixture. As the mixture thickens, the dough will start to become shaggy. Once you can't swirl any more flour in this way, use a pastry scraper to start to fold the flour into the dough and knead it with the heels of your hands. Keep kneading and incorporating as much flour and parts that have broken off into the main dough ball. This will take a good 10 to 15 minutes. The dough will

eventually start to soften and become smooth and elastic. Keep kneading for another 10 minutes. You can't overdo the kneading.

2   Form a tight dough ball and wrap it in plastic wrap. Let it rest for 30 minutes to an hour. (You can make the dough the day before and keep it tightly wrapped in the refrigerator. Bring it back to room temperature before you roll it out.)

3   *Make the filling:* Heat the oil in a cast iron or heavy skillet over medium-high heat. Add the onions and sauté until they start to turn brown at the edges, about 5 minutes. Add the ground turkey and cook, breaking it apart with a wooden spoon, until it's cooked through and becomes crumbly in texture, about 5 minutes. Add the minced sage leaves and continue to cook, stirring often, until the mixture becomes fragrant, about 3 minutes. Stir in the egg and the cream and cook just until the filling comes together, about 3 minutes. Season with the salt and pepper.

4   *Make the rice:* Meanwhile, combine the water, a pinch of salt, and rice in a pot. Stir well, cover with a lid, and bring to a boil. Reduce the heat and simmer for 45 minutes or until most of the rice kernels have opened fully, showing the white inside. Drain well, cover, and set aside.

5   *Make the tortellini:* Divide the dough into 4 equal portions. Lightly flour a clean work surface or a cutting board. Set your pasta roller to the thickest setting. Flatten a portion of dough into a disc (keep the rest of the dough covered so it doesn't dry out) and send it through the pasta roller. Repeat, rolling and gradually reducing the setting on the pasta roller to its thinnest setting, until you get the pasta sheet as thin as you can. Place the pasta sheet on a floured surface; cover with a cloth, and repeat with the remaining dough portions.

6   Cut each pasta sheet into 2-inch / 5-cm squares. Place 1 tsp / 5 mL of turkey filling in the centre of each square. With slightly wetted fingers, bring two opposite corners of each filled square together to form a triangle. Press the edges together to seal the tortellini. Then bring two points of the triangle together and press to seal (it should now resemble a tortellini). One point will remain. Repeat with the remaining squares. >>

7   Fill a large soup pot with 8 to 12 cups / 2 to 3 L of
    water and salt it generously (about a tablespoon).
    Bring to a rolling boil. Working in batches so as not
    to crowd the pan, drop in the tortellini and cook for
    about 4 minutes, just until the dough is fluffy and
    cooked all the way through. Using a slotted spoon,
    transfer to a bowl and cover. Set aside and keep
    warm. If the pasta starts to stick together, gently toss
    it in a drizzle of oil.

8   *Assemble the dish:* In a large skillet over medium heat,
    combine the cooked wild rice and the cream. Cook
    for about 3 minutes, just to warm through. Add the
    cooked tortellini and gently toss to coat. Season with
    salt and pepper. Serve hot with grated Parmesan (if
    using).

# BRINED AND ROASTED QUAIL WITH HIGHBUSH CRANBERRY COMPOTE AND HONEYCOMB

MAKES 2 SERVINGS | SPECIAL EQUIPMENT: 8-QUART / 7.5-L POT; FOOD MILL

The highbush cranberry (*Viburnum edule*) is a glossy red berry that grows abundantly in central Alberta woodlands. The berries are way too tart in the summer, but they sweeten up after freezing. In the late fall and early winter, when the berries are ready for picking, they are often described as having a funky and sweaty smell. You'll know them by their fragrance! They are also easiest to pick in the dead of winter, when all of the leaves have fallen and the red berries can easily be spotted. You can substitute commercial cranberries for highbush cranberries. While not exactly the same flavour, you'll get the same pucker and bright citrusy taste.

1   *Brine the quail:* At least 5 hours before you want to serve this dish, start brining the quail: Combine the boiling water, salt, and syrup in a large pot (at least 8-quart / 7.5-litre capacity). Add the cold water and pepper. Stir to combine. Place the quail in the brine, cover, and refrigerate for at least 4 hours.

2   *Make the cranberry compote:* In a small pot, combine the cranberries and honey. Cook over medium heat, stirring occasionally, until it reaches the consistency of a thick jam (add some water if it seems too thick), about 10 minutes. Run the compote through a food mill and discard the skins and pips. Set aside.

3   *Roast the quail:* When you're ready to cook the quail, preheat the oven to 450°F / 230°C (see Tip on page 241).

4   Remove the quail from the brine and pat dry with paper towel. Reserve a bit of the brine to use as a baste while roasting. Place the quail on a roasting rack that allows airflow under the birds. Roast in the preheated oven for about 10 minutes, and then reduce the heat to 400°F / 200°C. Continue roasting for about 10 more minutes, basting the skin with

FOR THE QUAIL

1 cup / 250 mL boiling water

¾ cup / 175 mL coarse kosher salt or 6 tbsp / 90 mL sea salt

¾ cup / 175 mL pure maple syrup

16 cups / 4 L cold water

1 tbsp / 15 mL freshly ground black pepper

2 whole quail, cleaned

FOR THE CRANBERRY COMPOTE

2 cups / 500 mL highbush cranberries (fresh or frozen)

1 cup / 250 mL good-quality organic honey (see page 134)

1 small (2 inches / 5 cm square) honeycomb

A few clusters of fresh highbush cranberries (optional)

A few sprigs fresh parsley, for garnish

the reserved brine once or twice, until the juices run
clear from the leg joints when pierced and the quail
reaches an internal temperature of 170°F/77°C.
Remove the pan from the oven and let rest, tented
loosely in foil, for about 5 minutes before serving.

5   Using a sharp knife, carve the breast meat and thighs
from the carcass. Place the breast and thighs from
one bird on each plate with a dollop of the cranberry
compote and a slice of honeycomb. Garnish with
a few fresh cranberries and some parsley. Serve
immediately.

TIP

If you are using a
conventional oven, you may
need to either cook the dish
a little longer or increase
the oven temperature by
25°F/4°C.

# ON EMOTION AND RISK

**ASK ME TO MAKE A DISH** based on an ingredient and I'm already bored. I need something more. Emotions are the engine that drives my creativity. Emotions make me a better cook, but emotions can shut me down, too. When I'm in a bad mood, I can't create. Most of the time, though, I use my emotions as a starting point for something new.

I'm happiest and most creative when going into uncharted territory. I try never to repeat myself. And in order to do that, I've learned that I have to be prepared to fail, because you have to take risks to create something truly new and exciting.

Writing a cookbook has meant wading into unfamiliar territory and taking a risk that people won't understand my food or that they won't get where I'm trying to go with it. And then there's just the self-doubt and the massive effort it takes to refine dishes and put my thoughts in some sort of order. Many times over the past few years, the dream of creating a book that documents my journey of progressive Indigenous cuisine seemed so far away. But now that the dream has become a reality, I hope that it inspires people to open themselves up to Indigenous cultures and that it creates positive emotions, enjoyed through food.

*"I've learned that I have to be prepared to fail, because you have to take risks to create something truly new and exciting."*

# WAR PAINT

MAKES 4 SERVINGS | SPECIAL EQUIPMENT: LATEX GLOVES

I created this dish for a culinary competition in Edmonton called Gold Medal Plates. I won, which allowed me to compete in the national Gold Medal Plates competition. I had some issues with my food prep getting smashed up in transit to the event, and unfortunately I didn't place well that day. However, I was proud to present War Paint to a big audience and this has become a very special dish to me. If I have a signature dish, this is it.

You'll need to start this dish the night before so you have time to soak the wheat berries.

### FOR THE WHEAT BERRIES

1 cup / 250 mL wheat berries

5 cups / 1.25 L Pheasant Broth (recipe
    page 280) or good-quality chicken
    broth

### FOR THE QUAIL

4 quail legs

¼ cup / 60 mL canola oil

1-inch / 2.5-cm piece fresh horseradish

### FOR THE RED PEPPER SAUCE

4 red bell peppers, seeded, cored,
    and cut into quarters

2 cups / 500 mL pure maple syrup

1 cup / 250 mL good-quality
    organic honey (see page 134)

¾ cup / 175 mL duck or bacon fat

1 shallot, finely diced

1 clove garlic, finely diced

2 small zucchini

4 fresh mushrooms (such as oyster,
    chanterelles, or morels)

Salt and freshly ground black pepper,
    to taste

1    Place the wheat berries in a bowl or saucepan and cover with at least 1 inch / 2.5 cm cold water. Soak overnight.

2    Using a fine-mesh sieve, drain the soaked wheat berries (discard liquid). Transfer the wheat berries to a deep pot. Add the broth and bring to a gentle boil over medium heat. Cover partially and cook until the wheat berries start to split their skins, about 1 hour (they will be tender but chewy). Strain the broth into a bowl and reserve. Cover and set aside the cooked wheat berries until ready to use. >>

3   Trim the quail legs of any fat and trim any edges so the bone looks nice and clean. Set aside.

4   In a small saucepan, heat the oil to 300°F / 150°C. Peel the horseradish (discard the outer skin), and then shave off 20 or more thin strips. Fry the strips for 2 minutes, until just crispy. Using a wire-mesh scoop or slotted spoon, transfer to paper towel to drain. Set aside.

5   Poach the red peppers in a saucepan of simmering water over low heat for 5 to 10 minutes, just until softened but still vibrant. Using a slotted spoon, transfer to a bowl and set aside to cool. Once cool enough to handle, peel off the skin and discard.

6   Place the peeled peppers in a blender with a few tablespoons of the reserved broth from the wheat berries. Blend until smooth. Transfer to a saucepan and add the maple syrup and honey. Cook over a low heat, stirring occasionally, until the liquid is reduced by half and coats the back of a wooden spoon (this sauce needs to be thick and sticky; if it's runny, simmer until it achieves the right consistency). Strain through a fine-mesh sieve into a bowl (discard solids). Set aside.

7   Place the duck fat in a heavy pot or frying pan, and heat to 142°F / 61°C. Place the quail legs in the pan and cook for at least 20 minutes, until medium-rare (155°F / 68°C) or a little longer to cook them all the way through. Transfer the cooked legs to a plate lined with paper towel. Season with salt and pepper.

8   Pour all but a couple of tablespoons of the fat from the pan into a bowl and set aside. Heat the remaining oil in the pan over medium heat. Add the finely diced shallot and garlic, and cook gently for about 15 minutes, until fragrant. Add ¼ cup / 60 mL of the reserved fat, and stir in the cooked wheat berries. Sauté until warmed through. Season with the salt and pepper. Keep warm.

9   Preheat a grill to 400°F / 200°C. Cut the zucchini on the diagonal into ½-inch- / 1-cm-thick slices. If you are using chanterelles or oyster mushrooms, cut them in half lengthwise. Brush the hot grill with oil. Cook the zucchini and the mushrooms until tender, turning halfway through, about 6 minutes total. Season with salt and pepper. Set aside.

10  Place the red pepper sauce in a large shallow pan. Wearing a latex glove, dip the flat of your hand in the sauce and gently make a handprint on each of four serving plates. Place about 3 tbsp / 45 mL of warm wheat berries on each handprint. Arrange the grilled mushrooms and 1 or 2 slices of grilled zucchini on top of each mound of wheat berries. Angle a quail leg on top of each serving and place 4 or 5 horseradish slices alongside. Serve immediately.

# BONE MARROW WITH SMOKED CHEESE, RYE TOAST, AND A TOMATO CUCUMBER "TARTARE"

MAKES 4 SERVINGS

Marrow is the fatty centre of large bones. It's where blood cells are produced and is packed with iron, zinc, calcium, fatty acids, and vitamin A, among other things. So many cultures revere marrow, and Indigenous communities in Canada are no different.

I like this simple preparation of broiling it with grated smoked Swiss cheese and serving it with a side of toasted rye bread and some chopped tomatoes for some acidity.

You'll likely only be able to source beef bones with marrow, which is okay. Just make sure that you trust your butcher and the source of the bones is wholesome and healthy.

### FOR THE BONE MARROW

8 halves of femur bones, marrow intact, cut lengthwise into 4- to 5-inch / 10- to 13-cm lengths

1½ cups / 375 mL grated smoked Swiss cheese

Fleur de sel, to taste

10 to 12 slices rye bread, for serving

2 tbsp / 30 mL butter, for buttering toast

### FOR THE TOMATO AND CUCUMBER TARTARE

1 Roma tomato

½ cup / 125 mL diced English cucumber

¼ cup / 60 mL diced red onion

1 green onion, finely sliced

1 tsp / 5 mL finely minced garlic

1 tsp / 5 mL finely chopped fresh parsley leaves

1 tsp / 5 mL olive oil

1 tsp / 5 mL red wine vinegar

½ tsp / 2.5 mL salt

1   *Cook the bones:* Preheat the oven to 400°F / 200°C (see Tip on page 250). Line a rimmed baking sheet with parchment paper.

2   Place the bones marrow-side up on the prepared baking sheet. Sprinkle cheese evenly over the bones. Bake in the preheated oven for 10 to 15 minutes, until the marrow is bubbling slightly close to the bone but still pink right in the middle, and the cheese is a golden brown (the cooking time will depend on the size of the bones). Check the marrow for doneness with a toothpick: When it's done, the marrow will start to come away from the bone (remove from the oven before it starts to run). Remove the pan from the oven, season with fleur de sel, and set aside until cool enough to handle. >>

&gt;&gt;

3   *Toast the bread:* Toast the rye bread in a toaster or in the same hot oven (watching it very carefully so as not to burn). Spread lightly with butter. Cut toasts on the angle.

4   *Make the tartare:* Cut the tomato in half widthwise. Using your hands, squeeze out the juice and as many of the seeds as you can. Dice the tomato. Combine the diced tomato, cucumber, red onion, green onion, minced garlic, parsley leaves, oil, vinegar, and salt in a mixing bowl. Mix well.

5   To serve, place 2 bones on each serving plate with a few slices of buttered rye toast and a small bowl of the tomato and cucumber tartare. Serve hot.

---

**TIP**

If you are using a conventional oven, you may need to either cook the dish a little longer or increase the oven temperature by 25°F / 4°C.

---

# BISON TARTARE WITH DUCK-FAT-FRIED POTATO CHIPS

MAKES 2 TO 4 SERVINGS | SPECIAL EQUIPMENT: HEATPROOF COOKING THERMOMETER;
5-INCH / 13-CM RING MOLD AND 3-INCH / 7.5-CM RING MOLD (OPTIONAL)

Here's a winter version of steak tartare, with the added richness of egg yolk and the decadence of duck-fat-fried potato chips. Because you will be serving and eating this bison meat raw, use only top-quality boneless bison rib-eye, trimmed of silver skin and any fat. Tell your butcher you intend to serve it raw.

1   *Cook the egg:* Place the egg (still in its shell) in a small pot with enough water to cover. Attach the thermometer to the side of the pot, turn on the heat, and slowly bring up the water temperature to 145°F / 63°C. Cook the egg at that temperature for 1 hour. Take the egg out of the water and let it cool on the counter if you're going to use it soon. (You can cook the egg a day or so ahead of time and refrigerate until ready to use. Alternatively, you can also sous vide the egg; see page 31.)

2   *Make the potatoes:* In a deep pot over medium-high heat, bring the duck fat up to 300°F / 150°C.

3   Meanwhile, using a mandoline or your precision knife skills, slice the fingerling potatoes lengthwise as thinly as possible (⅛ inch / 3 mm is ideal). Working in batches, fry the sliced potatoes until they're golden brown and the fat stops bubbling around the edges, about 5 minutes. Using a wire-mesh scoop or slotted spoon, transfer to paper towel to drain. Season generously with about ½ tsp / 2.5 mL salt.

4   *Make the tartare:* Combine the chopped bison, garlic shallot mix, mustard, and capers in a bowl. Stir well.

>>

## FOR THE TARTARE

1 egg

1 × 3 oz / 85-g bison rib-eye, finely chopped

2 tbsp / 30 mL Minced Garlic and Shallots in Oil (recipe page 282)

2 tbsp / 30 mL grainy mustard

2 tbsp / 30 mL capers, rinsed, drained, and finely chopped

## FOR THE POTATOES

3 cups / 750 mL duck fat, for frying (approx.)

4 fingerling potatoes, unpeeled

1 tsp / 5 mL coarse kosher salt, divided

Several pea shoots for garnish

½ tsp / 2.5 mL finely chopped fresh parsley or chives, for garnish (optional)

>>

5   *Assemble the dish:* If you have ring molds, lightly oil
the inside of the larger mold and the outside of the
smaller mold with a swipe of canola oil. Arrange
them with the smaller ring mold inside the larger
one. Fill the space in between the two molds with
bison tartare and press firmly on a nice presentation
platter. Gently remove the rings. If you don't have
ring molds, use your hands to shape a patty for a
more rustic presentation.

6   Peel the shell from the cooled egg, and then remove
the cooked white. Holding the yolk over the tartare,
pierce the yolk and let it ooze out over the meat.

7   Arrange the potato chips around the tartare.
Garnish with the remaining salt and pea shoots, or
alternatively with chopped parsley or chives. Serve
immediately.

# PASTA WITH BISON "RAGÙ"

MAKES 4 TO 6 SERVINGS

My version of this classic Italian dish is made with bison and, of course, tomatoes, which are both native to the Americas and Indigenous communities. The long simmer requires patience but the results are well worth it.

1   Set a heavy-bottomed pot over high heat and heat the oil until it shimmers. Add the carrot, onion, and celery, and cook, stirring occasionally, for 8 to 10 minutes, until the carrot and celery are very soft and the onion is translucent.

2   Add the ground bison, breaking it up with a wooden spoon. Add the bay leaves. Cook until the meat is no longer pink, about 10 minutes. Season with the salt and pepper. Stir in the tomato paste, stewed tomatoes, and bison broth. Reduce the heat to a simmer and partially cover with a lid to allow some venting. Let simmer for about 30 minutes, stirring occasionally. If it starts to look dry, add a bit more bison broth or water (you want a fairly thick sauce, not soupy). Remove the bay leaves and discard them.

3   Meanwhile, fill a deep pot with cold water and 1 tbsp / 15 mL salt. Bring the water to a boil and cook the pasta according to the package instructions (until al dente). Strain with a colander. Add the pasta to the sauce while it's piping hot and carefully toss to coat.

4   Divide evenly between deep plates or serving bowls. Sprinkle with Parmesan cheese and serve immediately.

2 tbsp / 30 mL olive oil

1 large carrot, finely diced

½ medium onion, finely diced

1 rib celery, finely diced

1 lb / 450 g ground bison

2 bay leaves (fresh or dried)

1 tsp / 5 mL each salt and freshly ground black pepper, or to taste

1 small can (5.5 oz / 156 mL) tomato paste or ¾ cup / 175 mL homemade Tomato Paste (recipe page 281)

1 can (14 oz / 398 mL) stewed tomatoes

1 cup / 250 mL Bison Bone Broth (recipe page 276)

1 tbsp / 15 mL salt

1 lb / 450 g good-quality dried pasta (see Tip)

4 to 6 tbsp / 60 to 90 mL freshly grated Parmesan cheese

---

**TIP**

If you buy European pasta, it will likely come in a 500-g bag. Go with it. You'll have someone who wants a bit more than the others.

# BISON TENDERLOIN WITH FINGERLING POTATOES AND QUICK-PICKLED CABBAGE

MAKES 4 SERVINGS | SPECIAL EQUIPMENT: ROASTING PAN WITH ROASTING RACK; ROASTING THERMOMETER; 4-QUART / 1-L HEATPROOF CONTAINER

Grassfed bison tenderloin is such a treat. You really don't need to do anything special to it other than cook it to medium-rare. Here I'm pairing it with potatoes fried in butter and oil, and crunchy, sharp quick-pickled cabbage — the perfect companions to this premium part of such an important animal in Indigenous Prairie culture.

1   About an hour before cooking, remove the bison tenderloin from the refrigerator and cover loosely with aluminum foil to bring it to room temperature.

2   Place the fingerling potatoes in a large pot and cover with cold water. Add a pinch of salt and bring to a boil over high heat. Reduce the heat to medium-high and boil gently for 30 minutes, until a toothpick or sharp knife inserted into the centre of a potato slides in easily and comes out clean (cooking time will depend on the size of the potatoes). Drain well and cover to keep warm.

3   Meanwhile, in a soup pot, combine the red wine, ½ cup / 125 mL sugar, and bison broth. Bring to a vigorous boil over medium-high heat and cook for 45 minutes, stirring occasionally. Reduce the heat to medium and cook for another 10 to 15 minutes, until the liquid is reduced to a thick, dark, glossy syrup (you should end up with about 1 cup / 250 mL). Watch closely at the end to avoid burning. Remove the pan from the heat and set aside. >>

1 × 1-lb / 450-g bison tenderloin

8 fingerling potatoes, unpeeled and halved lengthwise

Salt, to taste

1 × 25-oz / 750-mL bottle dry red wine

1½ cups / 375 mL granulated sugar, divided

4 cups / 1 L Bison Bone Broth (recipe page 276)

¼ head green cabbage

1 cup / 250 mL white wine

1 cup / 250 mL rice vinegar

Salt and freshly ground black pepper, to taste

1 tbsp / 15 mL olive or canola oil

1 tbsp / 15 mL butter

Fleur de sel, to finish

½ cup / 125 mL tightly packed watercress, leaves and stems, for garnish

4    Shred the cabbage with a mandoline on the thin setting (about ⅛ inch / 3 mm thick). Transfer the shredded cabbage to a heatproof container. Set aside.

5    Preheat the oven to 425°F / 220°C (see Tip).

6    Combine the white wine, rice vinegar, remaining sugar, and 1 tbsp / 15 mL salt in a pot and bring to a boil. As soon as it boils, remove the pan from the heat and pour the mixture over the sliced cabbage (the cabbage tends to float, so weigh it down with a plate or something heatproof). Set aside to cool.

7    Pat the tenderloin dry with a paper towel and season it generously with salt and pepper. Place it on a rack in a roasting pan, uncovered (you want air circulating under as well as around the meat). Roast in the preheated oven for 30 to 40 minutes, until the internal temperature reads 130°F / 54°C (for medium-rare). Remove the pan from the oven and transfer the meat to a cutting board. Tent with aluminum foil and let rest for about 10 minutes (the internal temperature will rise a few degrees, to about 140°F / 60°C, while resting).

8    Meanwhile, combine the oil and butter in a large skillet over medium-high heat and heat until it shimmers. Place the fingerling potatoes cut-side down in the hot oil and fry until golden brown on the bottom, about 5 minutes. Transfer the fried potatoes to a plate (reserve the pan), season with a pinch of salt and pepper, and cover with foil to keep warm.

9    Add the cabbage to the reserved pan and cook over medium heat, stirring occasionally, until golden brown. Season with salt and pepper, cover, and keep warm.

10   Reheat the red wine bison broth reduction over medium heat, just for a few minutes.

11   To serve, put about ½ cup / 125 mL of the warm cabbage on each plate. Place 4 halves of potatoes on top of each serving. Drizzle with about 2 tbsp / 30 mL of red wine bison broth syrup. Using a sharp knife, cut the tenderloin into 1-inch / 2.5-cm rounds. Divide evenly among the serving plates. Season with some fleur de sel and 3 to 4 leaves of watercress. Serve immediately.

---

**TIP**

If you are using a conventional oven, you may need to either cook the dish a little longer or increase the oven temperature by 25°F / 4°C.

---

# MOOSE ROAST WITH BOILED POTATOES

MAKES 4 TO 6 SERVINGS

Moose is a large but shy northern animal, weighing 800 to 1400 lbs / 363 to 635 kg (bulls can be even heavier). Its territory ranges from the 60th parallel to the Arctic Ocean. It has long been a source of food (moose nose soup is a traditional dish that many people still enjoy). Its hide is used for clothing, especially moccasins. Its bones and antlers have been used for utensils.

My dad jokes that his favourite food is "good old slough-fed moose," and he loves it with simple boiled potatoes. And you know what? That's the best way to eat this. I love making this dish for my dad.

1   Preheat the oven to 325°F / 170°C (see Tip on page 260).

2   Sprinkle all sides of the moose roast with salt and pepper. In a heavy or cast iron pan, heat the oil over medium-high heat. Sear the roast for 2 minutes on each side (just enough to form a nice brown crust on all sides). Transfer to a braising pan, baking dish, or Dutch oven. Add the bison broth, garlic, bay leaf, peppercorns, and tomato paste. Cover, place in the preheated oven, and braise for about 2 hours or until the meat reaches an internal temperature of 145°F / 63°C.

3   Meanwhile, put the potatoes in a pot with enough water to cover. Add a big pinch of salt, cover with the lid, and bring to a boil over high heat. Reduce the heat and simmer for 20 to 40 minutes, until fork-tender (cooking time depends on the size of the potatoes). Drain well. Add the butter and finely chopped herbs, and stir to coat the potatoes evenly. Season with salt and pepper. Keep warm on the stove, covered. >>

1½ tsp / 7.5 mL salt, divided

½ tsp / 2.5 mL freshly ground black pepper

1 × 2.2-lb / 1-kg moose roast, shoulder, or cross rib (approx.)

¼ cup / 60 mL canola oil

4 cups / 1 L Bison Bone Broth (recipe page 276)

1 garlic bulb, cloves separated

1 bay leaf (fresh or dried)

1 tbsp / 15 mL whole black peppercorns

¼ cup / 60 mL Tomato Paste (recipe page 281) or store-bought tomato paste

3 large Yukon Gold potatoes, peeled and cut into quarters

¼ cup / 60 mL butter

3 sprigs fresh parsley, leaves only, finely chopped

2 sprigs fresh rosemary, leaves only, finely chopped

5 sprigs fresh thyme, leaves only, finely chopped

Salt and freshly ground black pepper, to taste

>>

4   When the roast is ready, transfer it to a cutting board
    with a trough (to collect the juices). Tent loosely
    with aluminum foil and let rest for 10 minutes.
    Meanwhile, if there's any fat floating on the surface
    of the braising liquid, skim it off using a large spoon.
    Put the pan back on the stove and bring to a boil,
    stirring to scrape up any browned bits at the bottom.
    Simmer for about 10 minutes, or until the liquid is
    the consistency of gravy.

5   Serve the roast family-style on a large platter or
    cutting board with the potatoes and a small gravy
    boat of the reduced pan juices.

---

**TIP**

If you are using a
conventional oven, you may
need to either cook the dish
a little longer or increase
the oven temperature by
25°F / 4°C.

---

# IRON POT STEW

MAKES 6 TO 8 SERVINGS

Stews are great one-pot winter dishes, especially for a crowd. Serve with toast. It's simple, comfortable, and homey.

1    Take the bison shoulder out of the fridge about 30 minutes before cooking to bring to room temperature.

2    In a cast iron pot, heat ¼ cup / 60 mL of the oil over medium-high heat. Add the sausage and fry until it begins to brown, about 5 minutes. Transfer the sausage to a plate. To the same pan, add the bison and sear all over, 5 to 7 minutes. Transfer the bison to a plate. Cut the sausage into ½-inch / 1-cm pieces. Cut the bison into bite-size pieces. Set aside.

3    Pour off the fat from the pan and return the pan to the stove over medium heat. Add the remaining ¼ cup / 60 mL of the oil. Toss in the leek, onion, garlic, red pepper, mushrooms, and parsley and cook until all the vegetables are soft, 8 to 10 minutes.

4    Return all of the browned meat to the pan and increase the heat to high. Stir in the broth, reduce the heat, cover, and simmer for 15 to 20 minutes, until thickened somewhat. Season with salt and pepper.

5    Toast the bread and brush it with flax oil. Divide the stew evenly among serving bowls and serve with the toast alongside.

---

1 × ½-lb / 225-g bison or beef shoulder

½ cup / 125 mL canola oil, divided

1 lb / 450 g elk or game sausage

1 leek, finely diced

1 white onion, minced

3 tbsp / 45 mL minced garlic

1 red bell pepper, seeded and finely diced

2 cups / 500 mL roughly chopped shiitake mushrooms

1 bunch fresh parsley, leaves and some stems, finely chopped

3 cups / 750 mL Bison Bone Broth (recipe page 276) or good-quality chicken broth

Salt and freshly ground pepper, to taste

6 to 8 slices rye bread, for serving

3 to 4 tbsp / 45 to 60 mL cold-pressed flax oil, for brushing on toast

# SALT-ROASTED BEETS

MAKES 6 BEETS | SPECIAL EQUIPMENT: RUBBER OR LATEX GLOVES (OPTIONAL)

There's a huge salt bed on the Canadian Prairies. It angles from southwestern Manitoba through central Saskatchewan and then up to northern Alberta. A salt plant in Elk Point, Alberta, produces up to 200 tons of salt per day. And beets with dill is a classic Prairie food pairing. This dish is an homage to those three important ingredients — salt, beets, and dill — and my home province.

Salt-roasting steams the beets right in their skins, giving them a satiny smooth texture and intense flavour. Salt-roasted beets are great sliced and sprinkled with fresh dill, cubed on a charcuterie plate, or sliced and tossed in a green salad with goat cheese. Use the method below for the beet salad on page 121, or as a side for fish, chicken, bison, or beef dishes.

1 Preheat the oven to 400°F / 200°C (see Tip). Cover the bottom of an 8- by 6-inch (20- by 15-cm) loaf pan or a 9-inch / 23-cm round cake pan with a layer of salt that is approximately ¼ inch / 0.5 cm deep.

2 Using a sharp knife, trim the beet greens so that about 1 inch / 2.5 cm of the leaf stalk remains and remove the small root tail at the bottom of each beet. Set aside.

3 Using a stand or electric mixer, whip the egg whites to about half-stiffness (you want them to flow nicely and not be too stiff). Fold in the chopped dill.

4 Holding the beets by the tops, roll them in the egg white mixture, and then stand them up in the bed of salt in the pan.

5 Carefully pour the remaining salt around the beets until just the very tops are exposed. Bake in the preheated oven for about an hour, until the beets are cooked but still firm (test by sticking a sharp paring knife into one of the larger beets: It should go in fairly easily). Remove the pan from the oven and let the beets rest for about 15 minutes or until they are cool enough to handle.

3 lbs / 1.4 kg coarse kosher salt

6 medium beets

4 egg whites

⅓ cup / 80 mL chopped fresh dill fronds

> **TIP**
>
> If you are using a conventional oven, you may need to either cook the beets a little longer or increase the oven temperature by 25°F / 4°C.

6   Once the beets are cool, shake off the excess salt and, using your hands, peel off and discard the skins (you may want to wear rubber or latex gloves to avoid staining your hands).

# BEET-STAINED POTATOES
# WITH HORSERADISH CREAM

MAKES 4 SERVINGS

My family had a huge garden on our acreage in central Alberta, so of course we grew lots of potatoes and beets. After my dad, my brother, and I built a large root cellar, Mom would store our garden produce in there from harvest throughout the winter.

Plain potatoes, gently boiled in water, are very popular on the dinner tables in many Indigenous communities. This recipe is a fusion of that satisfying staple food and the memory of my family's root cellar, packed with beets and other items that kept well all winter, like carrots, turnips, and even horseradish.

### FOR THE HORSERADISH CREAM

4 oz / 115 g fresh horseradish root, peeled

1 cup / 250 mL whipping (35%) cream

1 cup / 250 mL half-and-half (10%) cream

1 tbsp / 15 mL cornstarch

1 tbsp / 15 mL cold water

1 tsp / 5 mL salt

### FOR THE POTATOES, BEETS, SHALLOTS, AND BABY KALE

3 to 4 large Yukon Gold potatoes, peeled

1 cup / 250 mL whipping (35%) cream

3 cups / 750 mL cold water

Pinch of salt

2 medium beets, trimmed and peeled

2 large shallots

Fleur de sel, to taste

Neutral-flavoured cooking oil (such as canola), for frying (about 1 cup / 250 mL)

A few leaves of baby kale

Freshly ground black pepper, to taste

¼ cup / 60 mL chopped fresh dill fronds

1   *Make the horseradish cream:* Using the large holes on a box grater, grate the horseradish into a small saucepan. Stir in the whipping cream and half-and-half. Cover and refrigerate for 1 hour.

2   Set the saucepan over medium-low heat and bring the horseradish mixture to a simmer. Cook for about 30 minutes (don't let it boil). Using a fine-mesh sieve, strain the cream into a clean saucepan (discard the solids). Place the pan over low heat and bring to a low simmer.  >>

3   In a small bowl, stir together the cornstarch and water. Add to the cream, stirring constantly, and simmer for 15 minutes. Remove from the heat and set aside to cool. Cover and refrigerate until ready to use. (This can be done a few days in advance.)

4   *Prepare the vegetables:* In a pot, combine the potatoes, whipping cream, and water. Add the salt and bring to a gentle simmer over medium heat. Cook for 20 to 30 minutes, until the potatoes are just tender enough that you can insert a sharp paring knife into the centre (you don't want them so soft that they are starting to fall apart). Drain and set aside to cool.

5   If you have a juicer, juice the beets. Otherwise, purée the beets in a blender until liquefied, adding a bit of water if you need to. Pour the beet juice or purée into the pot with the drained potatoes. Toss to coat and set aside.

6   Preheat a grill to medium-high (about 400°F / 200°C) and brush it with oil.

7   Cut the shallots in half and remove the very inner layer, especially if it has started to sprout. This removes any bitterness from a sprouted centre and also creates a nice cup-shaped shallot. Place the beet-stained potatoes and the shallots on the hot grill and cook, turning occasionally, until the potatoes crisp up and the shallots start to soften, and both take on some grill marks, about 3 minutes per side. Remove from the heat and season with fleur de sel. Set aside.

8   Pour about 3 inches / 7.5 cm of canola oil into a small saucepan and heat to about 375°F / 190°C (it's hot enough when you start to see little rivers move quickly around on the bottom of the pan). Fry the kale leaves until they are just crispy and slightly golden around the edges. Using a wire-mesh basket or slotted spoon, transfer the fried leaves to paper towel. Season with a pinch of salt.

9   To serve, dollop generous spoonfuls of horseradish cream on a platter or a cutting board. Sprinkle with freshly ground pepper and a bit of fleur de sel. Arrange the grilled potatoes and shallots, and fried kale around the horseradish cream. Garnish with fresh dill.

# WINE-POACHED OKANAGAN PEARS WITH VANILLA MASCARPONE FILLING

MAKES 6 SERVINGS | SPECIAL EQUIPMENT: MELON BALLER

I don't use a lot of wine in my cooking, but British Columbia's hot and dry Okanagan Valley is home to some very good Indigenous-owned and -operated wineries, and it would be a shame not to celebrate that. One of the best known ones is Nk'Mip (pronounced Inka-MEEP) Cellars, which happens to be North America's first Indigenous-owned winery. It's on the Osoyoos reservation, home to the 500 members of the Osoyoos Indian Band. The wines regularly win accolades and awards, and I have been visiting there for a few years to collaborate with winemaker Justin Hall (Osoyoos Band). I also have family in the Shuswap area of the East Kootenays in British Columbia, and family vacations were all about eating up as much tree fruit as we could stomach. This recipe is intended to bring back warm summer memories just when you need it most: in the cold, dark days of winter. The mascarpone is a lovely surprise in the centre.

If you can find it, use chestnut blossom honey in this recipe — chestnut is a classic winter solstice and Christmas flavour.

FOR THE POACHED PEARS

6 firm pears (e.g., Bosc or Anjou)

1 x 25 oz / 750 mL bottle sweet white wine (ideally a Riesling, Gewurztraminer, or Ehrenfelser)

2 cups / 500 mL water

½ cup / 125 mL pure maple syrup

⅓ cup / 80 mL good-quality organic honey (chestnut blossom, if possible; see page 134)

¼ cup / 60 mL white vinegar

2 tbsp / 30 mL dried juniper berries

2 x 3-inch / 7.5-cm cinnamon sticks

FOR THE VANILLA MASCARPONE FILLING

1 cup / 250 mL mascarpone cheese

2 tsp / 10 mL granulated sugar

1 tsp / 5 mL pure vanilla extract

FOR THE CINNAMON DUST

½ cup / 125 mL granulated sugar

¼ cup / 60 mL ground cinnamon

1   *Poach the pears:* Using a sharp paring knife, peel the pears and give the bottoms a trim so they sit flat in a casserole or stockpot big enough to accommodate them without too much extra space. Add the wine, water, maple syrup, honey, vinegar, juniper berries, and cinnamon sticks. Add a bit more water, if necessary, so that the liquid comes up to the top of the pears; it doesn't need to cover the stems. Place the pan over medium heat and cook at a bare simmer for about 20 minutes for Anjou pears or 30 or more minutes for Bosc pears, until soft. The traditional technique is to cut a piece of parchment in a round shape so that it can sit just on top of the pears as they simmer to keep them from browning and to help them evenly poach. Or you can simply baste the pears with the poaching liquid as they simmer.

2   Using a slotted spoon, transfer the pears to a bowl and set aside. Bring the poaching liquid in the pan to a boil and cook until the volume is reduced by a third and it reaches the consistency of syrup.

3   Meanwhile, using a melon baller or a sharp paring knife, remove the lower part of the core and the seeds by making a cavity in the bottom of the pear.

4   Place the cored pears in a container with a tight-fitting lid. Pour the syrup gently over the pears, cover, and refrigerate for at least 6 hours or overnight.

5   When ready to serve, remove the pears from the liquid and set them on a plate to dry off slightly.

6   *Make the vanilla mascarpone filling:* Meanwhile, combine the cheese, sugar, and vanilla in a bowl and stir until well blended. Spoon just enough of the mixture into the hollowed core of each pear to fill the space.

7   *Make the cinnamon dust:* Combine the sugar and cinnamon in a shallow dish. Carefully roll the filled pears in the cinnamon sugar until well coated.

8   Serve slightly chilled or at room temperature.

# WINTER BERRY SOUR

MAKES 6 DRINKS | SPECIAL EQUIPMENT: COCKTAIL SHAKER; MUDDLING STICK

Here's a celebration drink that contains antioxidants and vitamins from berries and features a pleasing tartness from verjus (a vinegar made from unripe grapes) as well as a woody, forest flavour from birch syrup (which nicely counterbalances the tartness of the verjus). If you can't find birch syrup, you can substitute pure maple syrup or even a good honey (see page 134).

1   In a tall cocktail tumbler, combine the berries, verjus, and syrup. Using a muddling stick, muddle the ingredients together until all the berry skins are broken and the mixture forms a thick purée. Add the water, put the lid on the shaker, and shake well. Transfer the tumbler to the refrigerator and let chill for about 30 minutes.

2   Pour the chilled purée through the shaker into a glass jar (to ensure all of the small seeds and pulp are caught, you can also pour it through a fine-mesh sieve); discard the solids.

3   Pour about 2 ounces / 60 mL per glass. Serve in fancy, festive stemware.

1 cup / 250 mL wild blueberries, mossberries, or saskatoons (fresh or thawed from frozen)

½ cup / 125 mL verjus

1 to 2 tbsp / 15 to 30 mL pure birch syrup, to taste

2 cups / 500 mL water

---

**TIP**

Verjus is a great non-alcoholic addition to sour mocktails. You can buy it in specialty food stores or order it online.

---

# PANTRY STAPLES

The items in this section are referred to throughout this book. These flavour boosters are in constant use in my home and professional kitchens. My hope is that as you cook through my recipes, you'll add these staples to what you already have on hand in your pantry and refrigerator — and that, slowly, they will permanently replace any store-bought broths, flavour bases, and condiments. The effort to make these pays off, trust me.

# BISON BONE BROTH

MAKES 5 GALLONS / 20 L | SPECIAL EQUIPMENT: 5-GALLON / 20-L STOCKPOT; LARGE COLANDER; 5-GALLON / 20-L FOOD-SAFE CONTAINER; AND LOTS OF FREEZER-SAFE RESEALABLE CONTAINERS

Bone broth, which is essentially a really good stock, is a bit thicker and richer tasting than most other broths. Bison bone broth is low in fat, high in protein, and packed with vitamins and minerals. The addition of tomato paste helps to break down the elastin and collagen in the bones as they simmer (it also contributes beautiful colour).

This recipe is definitely a bit of a project — the large quantities here (by weight) are geared toward professional chefs and culinary students — but afterward you can reward yourself with a freezer full of the most delicious and healthy bone broth you've ever tasted.

1   Evenly space racks in oven. Preheat the oven to 350°F / 180°C (see Tip on page 277).

2   Arrange the bones in single layers on rimmed baking sheets or in roasting pans. Roast the bones until they are medium dark in colour, about 1 hour. Remove the pans from the oven and brush three-quarters of the tomato paste onto the bones with a large pastry or basting brush. Return the pans to the oven and continue to roast until the bones are dark brown, another 45 minutes.

3   Once all of the bones are roasted, carefully transfer them to a large stockpot and set aside.

4   While they are still hot, place the roasting pans on your stove top and add about 2 cups / 500 mL water to the bottom of each pan. Turn the heat to medium-high and bring to a boil, using a spatula or flipper to scrape up all the drippings from the bottom of the pans. Carefully transfer the dark liquid to the stockpot.

10 lbs / 4.5 kg bison bones (knuckle bones, split and clean marrow bones, cartilage, etc.), trimmed of any fat (see Tip on page 277)

1 cup / 250 mL Tomato Paste (recipe page 281) or store-bought tomato paste, divided

2.2 lbs / 1 kg celery stalks and tops, roughly chopped

2.2 lbs / 1 kg onions, roughly chopped

2.2 lbs / 1 kg carrots, roughly chopped

2½ oz / 70 g fresh rosemary sprigs

2½ oz / 70 g fresh thyme sprigs

2½ oz / 70 g fresh parsley sprigs (curly or flat-leaf)

2 bay leaves (fresh or dried)

2 oz / 55 g whole black peppercorns

21 qt / 20 L water, divided

5    In a large bowl, toss the chopped vegetables with the remaining tomato paste (you may need to do this in batches). Arrange the mixture in single layers on rimmed baking sheets or in roasting pans. Roast the vegetables in the 350°F / 180°C oven until nice and dark in color, watching carefully so they don't burn (burnt vegetables taste bitter), 30 to 45 minutes.

6    Transfer the roasted vegetables to the large stockpot with the bones.

7    Toss in the herbs, bay leaves, and peppercorns. (If you wish, create a sachet by tying the seasonings in a cheesecloth bundle and securing it with butcher's twine. If you do this, remember to tie the sachet to the handle of the stockpot to make it easy to remove.)

8    Add 10½ quarts / 10 L of cold water to the stockpot. Cover the pot with the lid and simmer the mixture over medium-low heat for 10 to 15 hours. Remove from the heat and set aside to cool slightly. Strain through a large colander into a 5-gallon / 20-L food-safe container (reserve the solids), and refrigerate or keep cool. Return all the bones, vegetables, and herbs to the stockpot.

9    Pour another 10½ quarts / 10 L of cold water over the bones, roasted vegetables, and herbs in the stockpot and simmer again, uncovered, over medium-low heat for another 10 to 15 hours. Strain through a large colander into the 5-gallon / 20-L container with the first batch. Let cool, then portion the broth into smaller resealable containers. Allow ½ inch / 1 cm airspace between the lid and the broth in a 2-cup / 500-mL container, and 1 inch / 2.5 cm in a 4-cup / 1-L container. The broth will keep in the fridge for 3 to 4 days, and in the freezer for up to 6 months.

TIPS

Talk to your specialty butcher about bringing in bison bones. If they have bison meat available, chances are they can bring in the bones for you as well. For the marrow bones, ask your butcher to split them for you. (Try the Bone Marrow with Smoked Cheese, Rye Toast, and a Tomato Cucumber "Tartare" recipe on page 249.)

If you are using a conventional oven, you may need to either cook the dish a little longer or increase the oven temperature by 25°F / 4°C. Additionally, it's best to make this recipe in winter. Most homes don't have large enough refrigerators to cool a 20-gallon container, so in Canada we place the hot stock outside to cool before portioning it into smaller containers.

# The Holm Family and Strawman Farm: All-Natural Bison

Bob Holm used to be a drummer in a rock band. I love that he still dresses the part even though his days are now filled looking after a herd of bison and working with his wife, Lori, and their three sons on the family farm northwest of Edmonton (where they also have an indoor vertical strawberry farm and a commercial kitchen, among other things).

I met Bob when he approached me to buy the bison broth he makes in his on-farm commercial kitchen. We hit it off right away and have since become good friends.

I had been looking for a local supplier of a healthy, delicious broth — it takes a lot of time and labour to make a proper one. There are a lot of stocks out there that I could choose but because of my relationship with Bob, it makes sense for me to support him just like he supports me. (Bob and Lori cheered me on when I won the Gold Medal Plates competition in Edmonton and then travelled to Kelowna, British Columbia, when I got to compete in the national Canadian Culinary Championships against several of the best chefs in Canada in 2018.)

It's so interesting to watch Bob interact with his herd. To move the cattle from one pasture to the next, he simply walks along the outside of the fencing, hundreds of metres away from them. As soon as one of the bison spots him, the rest of the herd seems to go on alert and then will cautiously band together and keep their distance. Bob moves calmly so as not to start a stampede. Even so, a few will go from a walk to that ungainly gallop that bison have, but after a short while, they'll settle down and continue to graze and chew.

Bison are indigenous to the Prairies and don't require antibiotics, hormones, steroids, or other strange things that can be used when raising beef. Nor do you feed them grain at any time during their lives. With bison, you just let them graze on native grasses, just as they've been doing for thousands of years on the Great Plains. They also calve on their own, unassisted. As Bob says, "You just let bison be bison."

# PHEASANT BROTH

MAKES 1 TO 3 QUARTS / 1 TO 3 L, DEPENDING ON THE SIZE OF THE CARCASS

Pheasant broth seems a bit exotic, but the flavour surpasses chicken broth (especially most store-bought chicken broths). My recipe for Roast Pheasant with Acorn Squash on page 167 will provide the perfect carcass for what will undoubtedly become a pantry staple in your kitchen. You can also use a leftover chicken or turkey carcass, if you like. If using a turkey carcass, double or triple the amount of vegetables, peppercorns, and herbs called for to ensure good flavour.

1   Put the carcass in a large soup pot and add cold water to cover. Over medium heat, bring it slowly to a boil and then reduce the heat to a simmer. Cook for about 30 minutes, uncovered.

2   Tie the rosemary, thyme, and parsley together with butcher's twine. Add the herb bundle to the soup pot. Add the bay leaf, onions, celery, carrots, and peppercorns. Continue to simmer for 2 hours, uncovered.

3   Strain the broth into a large heatproof container to cool (discard solids). Let cool completely and skim off or remove any fat. Portion into resealable containers. Will keep in the fridge for up to 4 days and in the freezer for up to 6 months.

1 cooked pheasant (or chicken or turkey) carcass, mostly stripped of its meat and skin

Cold water, to cover

2 sprigs fresh rosemary

6 sprigs fresh thyme

6 sprigs fresh parsley (curly or flat-leaf), leaves and stems

1 dried bay leaf

1 to 2 medium onions, peeled and roughly chopped

1 to 2 celery ribs and tops, roughly chopped

1 to 2 carrots, peeled and roughly chopped

1 to 2 tsp whole black peppercorns

# TOMATO PASTE

MAKES 3 CUPS / 750 ML | SPECIAL EQUIPMENT: KITCHEN SCALE; FOOD MILL OR
FINE-MESH SIEVE

Make tomato paste when local, organic paste tomatoes — Roma, Amish, San Marzano — are field ripe, abundant, and economical. The taste is incomparable to the canned stuff and a little goes a long way. Because of the quantities used in this recipe, it's easiest to weigh out the amount of herbs and garlic needed. To keep the tomato paste from discolouring and to ensure its flavour stays fresh in the fridge, pour just enough olive oil over the top to cover it completely and then cover with a lid.

10 lbs / 4.5 kg ripe paste tomatoes

6 oz / 170 g (1 cup / 250 mL) olive oil

1 tbsp / 15 mL salt

2 oz / 55 g fresh rosemary sprigs
(about 20 6-inch / 15-cm sprigs)

2 oz / 55 g fresh thyme sprigs

2 oz / 55 g fresh parsley sprigs
(curly or flat-leaf)

4 oz / 110 g minced garlic

1   Evenly space the three racks in the oven. Preheat the oven to 350°F / 180°C (see Tip on page 264 for a note on oven settings). Line three rimmed baking sheets with parchment paper.

2   Cut the tomatoes in half lengthwise. Using your hands, squeeze out and discard as much of the juice and seeds as you can. Place the prepared tomatoes in a large bowl and toss with the oil. Divide the tomatoes evenly among the prepared baking sheets, sprinkle with salt, and roast in the preheated oven for about 1 hour (one pan per rack, rotating pans halfway through), until soft and caramelized.

3   In a large pot, combine the tomatoes with the herbs and garlic. Bring to a gentle boil over medium heat, using a wooden spoon to mash and break up the tomatoes. Cook, stirring occasionally, for about 45 minutes.

4   Take the tomatoes off the heat and let cool until you can pick out (and discard) the herbs as best you can. Working in batches, run the tomatoes through a food mill or push through a fine-mesh sieve using the back of a large spoon into a large pot (be patient and process the tomatoes until no further pulp and juice come through); discard the seeds and skins.

5   Place the pot over medium heat and bring to a boil. Reduce the heat and simmer for about 2 hours, until the tomatoes form a thick paste. Remove the pan from the heat and let cool completely. Divide the cooled paste into resealable containers. Keep one in the fridge for up to a week, and freeze the rest until ready to use.

# MINCED GARLIC AND SHALLOTS IN OIL

MAKES 1 CUP / 250 ML

This mixture of equal parts minced garlic and shallots in oil is a very versatile seasoning. I use it as a flavour base in so many of my recipes — from soups to roasts — that I always have some on hand in the fridge. Remember to secure the lid tightly when storing it, otherwise other items in your fridge will take on its distinct flavour.

1   Combine the minced garlic and shallots in a resealable container. Add enough oil to cover the mixture completely. Seal the container and refrigerate. Will keep in the fridge for up to a week.

½ cup / 125 mL minced garlic

½ cup / 125 mL minced shallots

Neutral-flavoured cooking oil (such as canola), to cover

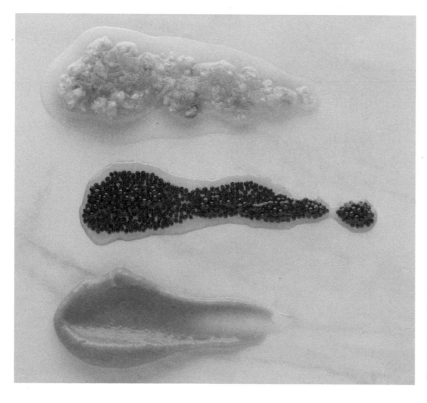

Top to bottom: Minced Garlic and Shallots in Oil; Sweet Mustard Seed Compote (recipe opposite); garlic purée (see page 209).

# SWEET MUSTARD SEED COMPOTE

MAKES ABOUT 1 CUP / 250 ML

I use this compote in my professional kitchen so often that it's become a signature of mine. The combined bite of the mustard seed, sweetness of the sugar, and acidity of the cider vinegar makes it a perfect match for charred meat and fish.

1   Combine the apple cider vinegar, honey, and pickling spice in a small saucepan. Bring the mixture to a boil over medium-high heat. Let boil gently for 30 seconds and then remove the pan from the heat. Let it cool completely, about 10 minutes, to fully infuse the liquid with the spices. Strain the mixture through a fine-mesh sieve. Discard the pickling spice solids and return the liquid to the saucepan.

2   Add the mustard seeds to the liquid in the pan. Cook over low heat, stirring occasionally (and don't let it boil, or the seeds will become bitter), for about 10 minutes, until the liquid has thickened to the consistency of honey. Watch it carefully during the last 5 minutes, as you want to pull the pan off the heat right away if the reduced liquid starts to turn brown (you don't want it to caramelize).

3   Once reduced, remove the pan from the heat and let the mixture cool completely. Transfer to a resealable container and refrigerate for up to a week.

½ cup / 125 mL apple cider vinegar

½ cup / 125 mL good-quality organic honey (see page 134)

1 tsp pickling spice (see page 166)

1 cup / 250 mL mustard seeds (black or yellow, or a combination of both)

**WHEN PEOPLE THINK OF THE CANADIAN PRAIRIES,** they often visualize vast fields of canola or flax. We grow a lot of mustard seed, too. I like that connection — of the mustard seed to where I live and cook — which is why my sweet mustard compote shows up in a lot of my recipes. You can use either yellow or black mustard seeds (ideally organically grown and purchased directly from the farmer or through a good local retailer), as suits your preference.

# PUFFED FRIED RICE

MAKES ABOUT 2 CUPS / 500 ML  |  SPECIAL EQUIPMENT: DEEP-FRYER; DEEP-FRY THERMOMETER

Guaranteed, this will be your next food addiction! I use this puffed rice as a salty, crunchy garnish for so many dishes in my restaurant. In this book, I sprinkle a little on top of my Leek-ash-coated Arctic Char with Squash Purée (recipe page 164), but once you taste it you'll want to have it on hand to garnish soups and salads, too. A word to the wise: It also makes a really great alternative to popcorn when watching TV — so make the full batch!

1   Bring the water, rice, and a big pinch of salt to a boil over high heat, and then stir well before covering with a lid. Reduce the heat and simmer for 45 minutes or until most of the rice kernels have opened fully, showing the white inside.

2   Line a baking sheet with parchment paper. Drain the cooked rice through a fine-mesh sieve and then turn out onto the prepared baking sheet. Let the rice dry and cool to room temperature, about 30 minutes.

3   In a deep-fryer, heat the oil to 350°F / 180°C. Alternatively, pour 2 inches / 5 cm of oil into a pot and heat over medium-high heat until the oil reaches 375°F / 190°C. (The smaller volume of the oil in the pot versus the deep-fryer accounts for the higher temperature. For shallow frying, allow the oil to come back up to temperature in between batches. Work in small batches so as not to crowd the pot.)

4   Fry the rice until it stops bubbling vigorously and is golden brown, 2 to 3 minutes. When each batch is done, use a wire-mesh scoop (known as a spider) or slotted spoon to transfer it to a clean paper-towel- or parchment-lined baking sheet. While the rice is still hot, sprinkle it generously with salt. Repeat until all of the rice is fried. Let the rice cool completely before storing, loosely covered, at room temperature. Tastes best when used within a few days.

3 cups / 750 mL water

1 cup / 250 mL wild rice, rinsed and drained

Neutral-flavoured cooking oil (such as canola), for frying

Salt, to taste

# BANNOCK

Bannock, also known as fry bread, always starts a conversation. It usually involves a critique of other people's bannock and detailed accounts of who makes the best! I always cringe when Elders come to the restaurant and order it — they are my harshest critics. However, I've tweaked my formula over the years and have finally come up with what I think is the perfect single recipe — at least for me — for the various ways you can cook bannock.

You may find my measures for the sugar and baking powder a bit unconventional (mixing tablespoons and teaspoons), but it's the best way to ensure the correct amounts are added (aside from weighing them out).

Bannock is very versatile as an accompaniment to soups, stews, dips, and spreads. This version is cooked over a hot grill, but you can make a thicker loaf and cook it in a cast iron pan over a fire or in an oven, or wrap bits of bannock around sticks to cook over hot coals. And of course, for a dessert, you can deep-fry small portions of bannock and sprinkle them with sugar (see recipe page 70).

1   Whisk together the flour, baking powder, sugar, and salt in a mixing bowl until well combined. Gradually add the water, blending it in with your hands. Be careful not to overwork the dough — it should just hold together. It will be a wet, shaggy dough but really resist overmixing it — at this point, you might think "this can't be right," but it is. Cover the bowl with a wet tea towel and set aside at room temperature for 30 minutes to rest.

2   Preheat the grill to high (400°F / 200°C).

3   Scatter some flour on a large, clean work surface. Divide the dough into 8 even pieces and shape into balls. Using a rolling pin, roll out each ball into a flat oblong about ¼ inch / 0.5 cm thick.

3 cups / 750 mL (15 oz / 425 g) all-purpose flour, plus extra for working the dough

2 tbsp + 1½ tsp (37 mL) baking powder (0.9 oz / 26 g)

2 tbsp + 1½ tsp (37 mL) granulated sugar (1.2 oz / 35 g)

¼ tsp / 1 mL salt

1½ cups / 375 mL water, at room temperature

Canola oil, for grilling

Fleur de sel, to taste

4    Brush the hot grill with oil. Brush one side of the oblong with a bit of oil and place the oiled side directly onto the grill. Cook for about 4 minutes or just until puffed up and the bottom of the bread has taken on brown grill marks. Brush the top side of the bannock with oil and flip over. Grill the other side for 3 minutes, just until browned. Remove from the grill. Generously season both sides of the hot bannock with fleur de sel. Serve warm.

**BANNOCK OR FRY BREAD** sometimes goes by its Michif (Métis language) name, galette. My grandfather made an excellent galette, which is more like a quick-rise loaf in our family, and now my dad is in charge of making galette on special occasions. I've included my dad's galette recipe on page 209, which is different from my recipe for bannock (opposite).

Some Indigenous people (including chefs) do not believe that bannock has a place in Indigenous cuisine, since it's a food adopted from early European contact, and the ingredients include processed white flour and white sugar. We acknowledge that it's controversial, and we suggest that it only be enjoyed occasionally. That said, it's everywhere in our communities, it's part of our celebrations, and many homes have favourite versions — including mine.

# AFTERWORD

BY JENNIFER COCKRALL-KING

There are two names on the cover, but most of this book is written in the first-person singular. Simply put, this is Shane's story and these are Shane's recipes. My role was to help Shane organize and express on the page what he's been doing in the kitchen for the past decade without really leaving much of a trace of myself. However, my part in this story is intertwined with Shane's.

Shane and I worked in the same industry for years. We knew of each other, but we didn't really know each other. A mutual friend, Michelle Peters-Jones, thought that I could help Shane get a cookbook idea off the ground and introduced us. Shane phoned me one afternoon in July 2014, and our conversation lasted for an hour and a half.

I was immediately drawn to his passion for the cultural roots of food, his lack of inhibition about dreaming big, and his determination to discover how his unique way of thinking about and cooking food fell in line with the land and the cultures that live on it. At first I felt I could only offer advice on writing a proposal and brainstorming some of the elements. But every time we talked, my excitement for his journey and what it could mean to Canada's food scene grew. Finally, after about a year of learning and laughing together, we knew that we had gone far enough down a road. If Shane would have me as co-author, I was all in.

Shane and I share a passion for food and how it connects people, as well as a genuine excitement for getting to know more about different communities. We both wholeheartedly believe that food is healing and that there are very few problems that good food can't fix, as long as we share it equally with one another. Needless to say, my friendship with Shane has grown as we've worked together to find the right words, recipes, and images to convey his ideas, his stories, and his vision.

I am honoured to help Shane write this story and to play a small part in a new understanding of Indigenous cultures and in this fresh excitement over a better way to think, live, love, and act toward one another on this land. I am grateful for the opportunity to be involved and even more grateful that my contributions have been so welcomed.

I have tried my best to convey how Shane captivates people with his creative and delicious culinary expressions — I find it impossible to call them merely recipes and dishes. Thank you, Shane, for the opportunity to join you on this important and exciting culinary journey. You are funny. You are fearless — or at least not limited by your fears. You are an artist and a believer in dreams. You are kind and trusting. And you are my friend.

*Jennifer Cockrall-King*

# ACKNOWLEDGEMENTS

Many people think that writing a book is a solitary activity, but nothing could be further from the truth. For four years, we were on the receiving end of so much generosity that a million thank yous will never be enough. People gave so abundantly of their time, knowledge, networks, and skills whenever we asked, which in turn inspired us to dream bigger and work harder. This book is the sum of those contributions.

The first thank you goes to Michelle Peters-Jones, a food-writing colleague in Edmonton, who saw the possibility of a book by Shane very early on, helped get the idea off the ground, tested some early recipes, and then brought Jennifer to the table. Thanks as well to the Alberta Foundation for the Arts, for an early grant to kick-start the process from idea to book proposal.

Thank you to Patti LaBoucane-Benson and Al Benson for bringing Sarah MacLachlan and Noah Richler to the restaurant at River Cree one night. And thank you to Sarah who instantly understood that she needed to acquire and publish this book.

To the staff and management at River Cree Casino & Resort, especially Vik Mahajan, VP and manager, and all the community members who allowed us the time and space to create this book. A special thank you to the past and present kitchen staff at SC Restaurant, whose many contributions are contained in the recipes and photographs of *tawâw*: Jesse Woodland, Christian Schmuland, JP Dublado, and the entire team of chefs and cooks who have joined us for the journey over the past four years.

To our cheerful and talented photographer Cathryn Sprague: You were up for any adventure, and your precision, skill, and artistry conveyed Shane's story beautifully. To Julie van Rosendaal, for your food styling crash courses, art direction, and recipe writing advice: We are forever grateful. For the final few frenzied days of capturing Shane's culinary artistry it was Paul Swanson and Aspen Zettel to the rescue while Cathryn was having her gorgeous baby boy.

Winnie Chen: You put in the long hours right beside us, cooking, jotting down recipes, helping with food styling and photography, on top of shouldering a million small tasks that were essential to getting this book finished. We are so grateful. And to Brad Lazarenko, for recipe testing assistance and a critical eye to smooth out some rough edges: thank you.

To the team at House of Anansi Press: What a privilege it has been to get to know you and to work together to create *tawâw*. Douglas Richmond and Maria Golikova, your passion for this book was evident from the start, and then you brought your editorial guidance, ideas, professionalism, and eagle eyes to bear. Speaking of eagle eyes, huge acknowledgements go to our excellent copyeditor, Tracy Bordian. Thanks also to proofreader Sarah Howden and indexer Ruth Pincoe. Endless and heartfelt gratitude to Dr. Arok Wolvengrey and Dr. Jean Okimāsis for the Cree-language proofreading and guidance. To Alysia Shewchuk, our book's designer, and to Holley Corfield, our publicist: Thank you for making sure this book receives the widest attention it possibly can.

For your support and contributions to telling this story, we are grateful for the words and thoughts of Marlene and Laurie Buffalo, Belinda and Dennis Chartrand, Cowboy Smithx, Ryan O'Flynn, Bob Holm, and Nakkita Trimble-Wilson.

Finally, to our personal teams of friends and family who offered encouragement when this project overwhelmed us, and to those who helped taste, test, and tweak recipes as they went from concept to plate to page: thank you.

# RECIPE INDEX

apples
  Bison striploin with celeriac cream
    and apple onion relish, 183–4
  Poached sweet and savoury autumn
    apples, 143
Arctic char, leek-ash-coated, with black
  garlic mushrooms and squash purée,
  164–6

bannock and galette, 129, 209, 287
  Bannock, 286–7
  Deep-fried bannock with saskatoon
    berries and birch syrup, 70
  Eggs with caviar and bannock, 29
  Galette with roasted garlic two ways,
    209–10
barley
  Smoked northern pike with barley,
    wild rice, and kale salad, 152–3
beans, dried
  Three sisters soup, 147–8
  White bean dip, 23
bee pollen, 94
  Fried smelts with wild rice, carrots,
    and wild leeks, 45–6
  Grilled octopus salad, 227–8
  Seared salmon with pickled carrots,
    cracked wild rice, and bee pollen,
    93–4
beets
  Beet-cured salmon with chanterelles
    and saskatoon sauce, 159–60
  Beet-stained potatoes with
    horseradish cream, 267–8
  Chocolate beet cake with saskatoon
    berries, 194–5
  Cold-smoked Haida Gwaii sablefish
    with sweet mustard compote,
    saskatoon berries, and beet tops,
    161–2
  Lamb chops with beets, 59–60
  Salt-roasted beet and goat cheese
    salad with candied pistachios,
    121–2
  Salt-roasted beets, 264–5
  Shaved root vegetable salad,
    187–8
  "Stained glass" salmon, 90

berries
  Soapberry whip on fresh berries, 130
  Winter berry sour, 272
  *See also specific varieties:* highbush
    cranberries, mossberries,
    saskatoon berries
beverages
  Highbush cranberry, mint, and
    maple sip, 72
  Iced Labrador tea, 133
  Wild ginger rosehip tea with honey,
    199
  Winter berry sour, 272
birch syrup, 142
  Deep-fried bannock with saskatoon
    berries and birch syrup, 70
  Poached sweet and savoury autumn
    apples, 143
  Winter berry sour, 272
bison
  Bison bone broth, 276–7
  Bison-broth poached halibut with
    grilled cabbage, whipped potatoes,
    baked kale, and roasted beech
    mushrooms, 154–5
  Bison liver and parsley soup,
    149–50
  Bison striploin with celeriac cream
    and apple onion relish, 183–4
  Bison tartare with duck-fat-fried
    potato chips, 251–2
  Bison tenderloin with fingerling
    potatoes and quick-pickled
    cabbage, 257–8
  Charcoal bison skirt steak with quick
    dill pickles and sweet mustard
    seed compote, 179–80
  Chopped bison with nettle pesto on
    rye toast, 67–8
  Iron pot stew, 263
  One-pot spaghetti squash, bison,
    and corn, 116–17
  Pasta with bison "ragù," 255
  Skewered bison strips, 114
Blackened cod with celeriac purée and
  crispy potato chips, 229–30
black garlic, 164
Braised venison shanks with a

mossberry black garlic glaze and
  herbed wheat berries, 191–3
Leek-ash-coated Arctic char with black
  garlic mushrooms and squash purée,
  164–6
  *See also* garlic
Bone marrow with smoked cheese,
  rye toast, and a tomato cucumber
  "tartare," 249–50
Braised venison shanks with a
  mossberry black garlic glaze and
  herbed wheat berries, 191–3
Brined and roasted quail with highbush
  cranberry compote and honeycomb,
  240–1
broths. *See under* soups
Brussels sprouts
  Kale and toasted pumpkin seed
    salad, 27–8

cabbage
  Bison-broth poached halibut with
    grilled cabbage, whipped potatoes,
    baked kale, and roasted beech
    mushrooms, 154–5
  Bison tenderloin with fingerling
    potatoes and quick-pickled
    cabbage, 257–8
  Pan-seared duck breast with creamed
    cabbage, blackened corn, and
    "confit" carrots, 171–2
carrots
  Pan-seared duck breast with creamed
    cabbage, blackened corn, and
    "confit" carrots, 171–2
  Seared salmon with pickled carrots,
    cracked wild rice, and bee pollen,
    93–4
caviar, 29
  Eggs with caviar and bannock, 29
  Smoked northern pike with barley,
    wild rice, and kale salad, 152–3
celeriac
  Bison striploin with celeriac cream
    and apple onion relish, 183–4
  Blackened cod with celeriac
    purée and crispy potato chips,
    229–30

# INDEX